Unexpected

Grit, Grace, and Life in Between

Trina Pockett

Endorsements

"*Unexpected* is a powerful, delightful, treasure, packed with truths! Trina shares her story and insights with such grit, wit and humor, I found myself laughing one minute, moved to tears the next, and inspired to change the world all the way through. Thank you, Trina for sharing your story with the world!"
  - Jana Alayra, Christian Music Artist & Speaker

"Trina Pockett is a survivor, a mother, a messenger of hope and practical wisdom, and — what's more —she is a true delight of a human being. Her story of grit and grace will be an encouragement and lifeline to women who long to remain faithful when they are feeling weak and broken. I think the world of Trina Pockett and love that she is sharing her story here."
  - Jennifer Grant, author of
    Wholehearted Living, Disquiet Time, MOMumental, and *Love You More*

"I've often said, 'At times, God has been silent, but He has never been absent.' After reading Trina's story, I was reminded of this, and assured of it, all the more. I'm so inspired by Trina's faith during God's momentary silence, and more importantly, her willingness to share it. I know this book will encourage you—wherever you are, whatever you are going through."

- Heather Palacios, Writer & Founder of *WondHerful.net*

This book is dedicated to the four most important people in my life...

Jeff, Caleb, Kate, and Noah.

You make life beautiful. Thank you for loving me in the grit and the grace.

Contents

I Am

I am **loving** and caring,
I wonder about the future
I hear the **beautiful** waves crashing together.
I see the many blessings I have.
I want to be successful and a woman of **Christ**.
I pretend to be a monster with my little brothers.
I feel **blessed** and happy.
I touch my parents.
I worry about my **friends**.
I cry when I lose a loved one.
I am thinking and wishing.
I understand my **purpose** in life and God has a plan
for me.
I say a **prayer** to God every chance I get.
I dream about brilliant colors and **wonders**.
I try to be the best I can at all I do.
I hope to impact everyone in my **life** for the best.
I am loving and **caring**.
I am understanding and sharing.

Michaela Aurora Zickuhr
July 2, 1992- April 19, 2009

Chapter One: Taking the Jump

"Courage is found in the most unlikely places." JRR Tolkein

I've cheated death twice in my life. The first time was at the tender age of eight.

I was a rascal. I grew up at the end of a cul-de-sac; spending most of my time playing catch until dark, learning to ride my bike without using my hands, and drawing hundreds of different hop-scotch patterns on the ground. Smells of eucalyptus filled the warm evening air as we took turns trying to hit a home run during the makeshift neighbor-hood baseball game. As the sun set behind the hills of our city, we each were called in, one by one, for dinner. I was usually covered in sweat and dirt and on the most unfortunate days, scrapes, scratches, and poison ivy. I didn't mind though. That's the price I paid for adventure. And I loved adventure.

Most girls were content playing with dolls and dressing up in heels. My sister Beth loved to wear dresses, brush her long blonde hair, and prac-tice her pirouettes around the house. I didn't have a graceful bone in my body and it didn't take long for me to realize that I wasn't cut out to be a dancer. I wasn't like most girls. My eyes were set on a differ-ent group of kids; the BMX bike gang. I watched those boys ride by on their street bikes—in forma-tion like a pack of wolves. Their bikes glistened in the sun as they passed by our mess of dolls. I want-ed *so* badly to be a part of that gang. I never knew where they were headed, but the bike gang was al-ways on the go. I was certain that they experienced epic adventures every day. I wanted to be a part of those adventures.

Being a girl lowered my chances of getting into the club. That, and the fact that my bicycle was purple with handlebar ribbons and a banana seat— complete with a basket on the front. I didn't exactly fit the BMX gang profile.

After months and months of watching the BMX gang ride by, I finally got the courage to ask if I could ride along. I didn't want to lead the pack (yet), I just wanted to peddle with them for a while. To my surprise, the leader of the gang gave me permission to ride along for the day. He probably thought that I would lose interest or that I wouldn't be able to keep up. Little did he know that it was my moment in time to prove that I was just as tough and just as brave as they were. I peddled my little heart out and followed those boys all over the neighborhood. The faster they went, the harder I peddled. The wind ripped through my hair and my calves burned, but I didn't care. I was free to ride with the cool bikes, explore new areas of our city, and chase adventure.

Day after day, I would run home from school, grab a snack, kiss my mom, and head out to get on my banana-seat bike. My agenda was the bike gang's agenda. Sometimes we would ride to the local market for penny candies. Other times we would make our way up to the community pool, but most of the time we just rode around the same three neighborhood blocks. We were like a family. I got the reputation as the cool younger kid, even though I was a girl. My days of peddling had given me a certain amount of credibility with those boys.

When the bike gang got tired of peddling, we found other activities to occupy our time. One summer day, we decided to build a dirt bike track. Once we had our general plans for the track, we each ran home to grab whatever makeshift tools we could find. Spatulas, buckets, bowls, and other random kitchen items were added to our tool pile. Using those tools we began to dig, sculpt, and shape our track. Mostly, I was the errand girl; retrieving shovels, picking up nails, and running home to get snacks for the workers. After what seemed a lifetime of work, we completed the track.

Everyone enjoyed their inaugural ride around the track, going over little mounds of dirt, turning on a dime, careening to a stop, impressing the crowd. Oddly enough, each biker avoided the colossal jump in the middle of the track. It was the elephant in the room, everyone knew it was there, but no one wanted to attempt it. If the jump was not executed correctly, it was certain death.

Where those boys saw fear, I saw an opportunity. Making that jump just might prove my abilities to the bike gang. I spoke before I had time to think about it. "I'll take the jump!" I shouted. Every head turned my way in disbelief. I, too, was shocked that I said it. I slowly walked forward allowing my bike to lead my reluctant feet. Panic started to sweep over me as I made my way to the front of the pack. The oldest boy asked me if I really wanted to attempt the jump. I think he was trying to give me an out. My pride (and youthful stupidity) kept me from running the other way. I gave an uncertain nod and in that moment my gang status jumped from low girl on the totem pole to cool kid. I was in my glory, basking up the accolades. Yes I, Trina Whipple, would be the first to attempt the jump.

The boys rallied around me, each giving me tips on how to execute the jump. Head up, pull up on the bike when you get to the edge, peddle into it. The older boys actually helped me do a dry run-through. I peddled to the ramp, and then they helped lift my bike into the air. I was soaring, well, almost. They gently set my bike on the ground and reassured me that I was going to do well. So, I peddled back to the top of the hill. A quiet hush fell over the crowd. I sat at the top of the hill giving myself a few final words of positive self-talk. I had no idea how this whole thing would end up, but I knew that I had to try. At this point, there was no backing out. I wanted to prove to the world that even eight year-old girls could be mighty.

So, I put one foot on the pedal and pushed down. With the momentum of the hill, I picked up speed quickly. Thoughts raced through my mind. Would I crash? Could I take a quick left and ride home? What if I actually landed this? I would be launched into neighborhood stardom. As the ramp got closer, I started to panic. What did the boys say? Lean into it? Lift the bike? I couldn't remember. My bike started to ascend on the ramp. My vision blurred and I could feel my heartbeat in my teeth. My front wheel started to roll over the edge. My hands gripped tight around my handlebars. Just as soon as my bike got close to the edge, I made a critical error: I leaned forward. It doesn't take a rocket scientist to figure out that when you lean forward your body and bike follow suit. I barely made if off of the ramp before my bike slammed into the ground below. It wasn't even a graceful fall. Legs and wheels were flopping every which way. A burst of dirt clouded around me. I had officially crashed and in my mind, failed.

I opened my eyes to see if I was dead. Nope, still alive. The shock of the crushing hurt settled in. I slowly untangled myself from the bike. The boys ran over to help me up, one even showed some tenderness by asking if I was okay. The best case was a perfect landing. The worst case was death. I landed somewhere right the middle of best and worst. My pride and my body hurt. I untangled myself from the bike and walked home—with blood running down my knees and a bruised ego.

As I write about that life experience, now I think of it in a completely different perspective. Not as a little girl who took the jump and failed miserably, but as a little girl who had the bravery to take the jump. Little did I know I would need that type of bravery later in life; the type of bravery that requires fearless peddling toward the unknown. Peddling toward what could be a perfect jump, or a miserable crash landing.

I needed that same brave heart on the day, many years later, when I was sitting in the hospital. The moment will always be seared into my memory. The words, "You have cancer," tore through the pages of my history. My memories would always be divided into chapters of before and after that day.

———

I was married at the tender age of 20. I stood in front of the minister and wholeheartedly promised my love for Jeff. I laugh now, because in those moments, I had no idea about the hard work that goes into marriage. I just knew that I was in love. I knew that eight months later Jeff and I would become parents. I know you just did the math. You subtracted correctly. We had a condensed amount of time to learn how to be married before turning into a family of three.

Those first few months of marriage were incredibly awkward, trying to figure out our dance of living together for the first time. Habits that seemed so spontaneous while dating suddenly seemed to be annoying. When did he like to eat dinner? Why didn't I hang up my towel? Who was in charge of the dishes? Those first few months were filled with endless scenarios of trying to blend two lives.

Our first real fight happened in the aisle of a grocery store. I walked gleefully up and down the aisle plucking items off of the shelf and placing them into the cart. Jeff decided to help himself to a few items. He grabbed a large jar of pickles and put them in the basket. What he didn't know about me was that I couldn't stand the taste of pickles. In fact, I despised pickles. From my perspective, I wasn't about to waste our grocery money on something I would never eat. So, I put the jar back on the shelf. Jeff asked what I was doing and I told him that I couldn't justify spending our hard earned money on disgusting pickles. Friends, I am aware of how selfish this sounds. My selfishness was clearly communicated to Jeff and he wasn't happy. He re-taliated in a way that I would send a clear message. He took my coveted pot-pies out of the cart along with my ice-cream, and walked down the freezer aisle to return them. Then I chose something of his to return. Our passive-aggressive food returns only lasted for a few minutes before our tempers got the best of us. Mean words spewed out. We left the store empty handed, but full of hurt feelings and bitterness.

Marriage was clearly hard work. Little by little we started to get the hang of it.

In the midst of building our marriage, we were also watching my belly grow with new life. It was an incredible time of wondering what our son would look like and whose traits he would have.

I did all of the mom research. I read *What to Expect When You're Expecting*, we signed up for Lamaze classes, we prepared the nursery, and I even stocked up on annoying (and totally embarrassing) maternity tops. Not too long ago, I found a picture of me about nine months pregnant wearing a white shirt with a teddy bear and the word "baby" underneath. A teddy bear? Seriously?

As we got closer to my delivery date, anticipation was quickly replaced with fear. I was about to have a baby, one that I would be responsible for. I would have to make sure that he could be protected from this seemingly cruel world. I would be the one to teach him everything that he knew. Thoughts raced through my head. *How could I be the one to be responsible for him? I didn't even know what I knew.* But time marched on, my belly grew, and the day finally arrived when our son wanted to meet the world.

What happened next is still a blur in my memory. My body entered into a profound state of knowing exactly what to do and when, even though all I was focused on was the pain. Oh, the pain! But, eight hours into the process, we finally got to meet our little man. Ten toes, ten fingers, and one heck of a scream. Caleb let the world know he had arrived.

Instantly I was propelled into parenthood. I guess I thought it would be like easing into a hot tub—one foot, then the leg, body, and finally, I'm in. But not parenthood. One minute the baby was nestled in my belly with everything he needs and the next minute, he's screaming out to the world, and I was the one who he was calling for.

I proudly assumed the role of mom. This was my boy and I was his mother. My heart expanded when I saw his little face. The love that I felt for him was overwhelming.

It's amazing to think how my life had changed within one year. My late night dates with Jeff turned into late night feedings with my son. I was surrounded by diapers and covered in stretch marks. The landscape of my life looked completely different.

Jeff and I did our best to get into the rhythm of life and parenting. Jeff worked, I stayed home with our son. This was a chapter of my life that included playgroups with moms who were much prettier & thinner than me—and had better strollers. Unfortunately, I didn't understand how comparison was fracturing me as a person.

I was desperate for real community. I wanted to know that other women had the same feelings and insecurities that I did. Jeff and I decided to get involved with a local church. On our first visit, a woman approached me and made small talk. She saw that I had a young son with me, and probably noticed that bags under my eyes. She asked if I was a part of MOPS (Mothers of Preschoolers). I had no idea what that was. She squealed with excitement over her MOPS group. She described meeting friends, enjoying a kid-free breakfast, and having real conversations with other moms. Conversations where she didn't have to act like she was perfect.

Honestly, this sounded exactly like the kind of group that I needed to attend. As a lonely young mom, I was tired of trying to look perfect and I was desperate for friends.

That next Tuesday, I decided to join. I walked into a room and realized that I had found my people. Real moms. Women of all ages in the same stage, trying to survive and thrive in mommyhood. I met amazing moms who shared the same parenting moments that I did; tired of feeling lonely at home, strains on the marriage, financial worries, never ending diaper changing. I found a community of women where I could be real and honest. I found a place to journey as a mom.

———

On January 1, 2000, most people were celebrating the fact that they had made it safely through Y2K, we were celebrating the fact that I was pregnant again.

There was so much to celebrate: new friends,

new baby on the way, life was moving along beautifully, or so I thought. I didn't realize the small signs around me that life wasn't as perfect as I thought. I constantly felt nauseous and fatigued. I wrote it off as the reality of being pregnant while chasing a toddler. My energy level waned, but I thought it was due to the cold that I couldn't shake. Then there was that little annoying lump that sat at the base of my neck. The baby wasn't the only thing growing inside of me.

I looked forward to the ultrasound appointment to find out the sex of our baby. We already had a little boy, so naturally, we wanted our second to be a little girl. I walked into the office hopeful that I would hear the words, "It's a girl." The technician squeezed a tube of jelly and a big glop landed on my belly. She took the scanner and rubbed it up and down over my belly. My husband and I stared at the black and white flickering screen. We were trying to make sense out of the images. Finally, a magical image of a lima bean shaped little baby showed up on the screen. Then to complete the experience, we could hear the sound of the heartbeat. The steady rhythm was more beautiful than any symphony.

The technician took her time taking measurements and assuring me that my baby looked healthy. I watched the screen intently to see if I could figure out the sex of the baby. I couldn't. Finally, she asked me if I wanted to know and I answered yes. Then I got my wish. I heard those three words. It's a girl! Joy filled my heart. My life couldn't be more perfect; a wonderful husband, my little boy, and now a sweet daughter. My life was on the fast-track to amazing!

The technician offered me a paper towel to wipe the jelly off of my belly. She helped me sit up, in those days, I needed help with the simplest tasks. Tying my shoes proved to be the biggest feat (no pun intended). The doctor entered the room to congratulate me and ask if I had any follow-up questions. I was quickly reminded of an annoying walnut-sized lump on the side of my neck. The lump didn't cause much pain, so I had dismissed it. I mentioned it to the doctor, and no sooner had I said the words when the doctor's face changed from comfort to concern. She reached up and felt the lump with her two fingers. She slowly moved away picking my chart up off of the counter.

Idle chat stopped and the air in the room

changed. Though I felt the awkward shift, I was still in elation at the news of being pregnant with a girl. The doctor jotted a few notes and then told me that she'd really like for me to meet with the ear, nose, and throat specialist. I told her that I would make an appointment first thing, to which she responded, "I mean right now." I was surprised by her concern and honestly a little annoyed. I wanted to get home and start calling my friends about the good news. I was having a girl!

But, I did what I was told and went to the office across the hall. Clearly, they knew that I was coming because I was immediately escorted into an exam room. A tall, athletic, young doctor, entered the room a few minutes later. He asked a few questions and then proceeded to feel the lump on the base of my neck. Same reaction: quiet withdrawal, then notes on the chart.

He said that he was uncomfortable with the lump and that he'd like to do an emergency biopsy. Those are two words that a pregnant woman does not want to hear; emergency and biopsy. The doctor was emphatic that a biopsy was incredibly important. This test would help rule out any serious conditions. I thanked him for his time and as I made my way up to the scheduling desk, I stopped in the hallway to make sense of the appointment. How did I go from elation to confusion in such short time? I felt like I had just heard a tornado siren and the wind was picking up momentum. Little did I know, I would be like Dorothy in the scene from the Wizard of Oz, trying to outrun the storm. In the toughest moments, I was certain the storm would win.

———

Intellectually I knew that I wasn't the only woman in the world to face daunting circumstances. As women, we are no strangers to adversity. It rears its ugly head in many ways: loss of a job, depression, relationship issues, illness, miscarriage, infertility, addiction, divorce, and so on. Women have struggled, fought, and trudged through hurts of all kinds.

As I considered other women who faced adversity, my mind turned to the story of Harriet Tubman. Her circumstances seemed insurmountably unfair. Harriet was born into slavery and lived her early years under harsh conditions; often whipped and beaten. At the age of 12, she took a severe blow to the head after she refused to help restrain a man who had attempted to escape. Even at that young age, Harriet was a fighter for justice. At the age of 30, fearing that she'd be sold to the South, she courageously decided to attempt an escape. Harriet's deep calling for freedom made her take action.

She faced adversity head on. Some may think that she had no other choice, but I believe that we always have a choice. She could have accepted her circumstances. She could have become bitter (I think I would have). She could have believed that slavery was all that was in store for her. But, instead she chose to make her move, knowing that the consequences of being caught would be a punishment ranging from a fierce beating to a painful death.

Imagine Harriet's feelings as she left the world that she knew; wondering every step of the way if she would be caught, trusting her safety to strangers, and journeying through the unknown.

Like Harriet, I've had many moments of uncertainty. I'm not saying that I understood what it was like for her to escape from a life of slavery. How can I even begin to understand that? But I have traveled uncertain roads, just as you have. Roads that turn to detours; finding a lump, or hearing that your husband is leaving you. The meeting with your boss when he tells you that he has to let you go because of budget cuts. The police officer at your door telling you that your child has been in a car accident. We all face unexpected moments and uncertainty in life.

Every woman has her own version of those moments. Some of you are walking that hard road right now. The question isn't *if* we will experience the pain and heartache of life, but *when* will we experience it and how we will respond to it? It seems that there are no easy answers in the midst of the storm.

Harriet Tubman has a story of extreme adversity, courage, and redemption. She did finally escape to Canada. For the first time in her life, she was a free woman. I often wonder what that moment was like for her. Was it disbelief? Instant tears? Pure joy? A combination of these feelings?

Harriet's story wasn't over when she reached Canada. The most beautiful part about Harriet's story wasn't the fact that she was finally free, but that she went back to help others. That's right. She knew that there were other slaves who also needed their freedom and she was going to do everything in her power to make that happen. Harriet Tubman led more than 300 slaves to freedom in the North.

Her willingness to revisit the most painful part of her life resulted in other people finding their own freedom.

We have the same opportunity with the adversity that we face. There are women who have experienced deep hurts and they need to find freedom. The truth is that our stories make a difference in the lives of others.

The adversity in life will challenge us, stretch us, and reshape us. But there is hope to be found in the process. We learn more about ourselves, our faith, and our hidden strengths.

Finding that lump forced me to find that brave little girl inside. The girl who was willing to face the ramp, pedal her heart out, and take the jump. In the moments of uncertainty, we all need to find that courage; the childlike faith that we will make it. And in the end, we will be stronger women because of what we faced.

Who knows how we'll land? What matters is that we keep peddling in life. So hop on your bikes and let's go.

Chapter Two: The Most Beautiful Stranger

"We must accept finite disappointment, but never lose infinite hope." Martin Luther King, Jr.

I've always been a little bit of a free spirit, an adventurer. When I was four, my parents gave the greatest birthday present a girl could ever want. Two things make this memory stick out in my mind: we were at my favorite restaurant, Burger King, and my birthday present was a brand new pink and purple powder puff Big Wheel. For me, it was like winning the final showcase on the "Price is Right." I ran over to my new wheels and parked my butt on the plastic seat. My fingers ran down the slick strands of glitter streamers hanging from the handlebars. I placed my feet on the wheels—ah, perfect fit. I was ready to hit the road.

As soon as we got home that day, I made my first loop around the cul-de-sac. I rode everywhere my mom would let me, which consisted of the cul-de-sac, the driveway, and on evenings when she was in the yard, I could venture to the end of the street.

That Big Wheel played a part in some of my happiest moments in my life, as well as one of my saddest moments. After a summer morning of riding my Big Wheel around the neighborhood, my mom called me in for lunch. I peddled my Big Wheel up to the gate and parked it next to a couch and a dresser. Yes, a couch and a dresser. I didn't think that those were odd items to be out in front of the house.

I flew through the front door, hopped up at the table, and waited for lunch. As usual I enjoyed a tuna fish sandwich and some potato chips. That was a staple meal when I was a kid. I washed it down with a splash of lemonade and headed back out for my afternoon adventure. Nothing could have prepared me for what I was about to see. The couch, the dresser, and my Big Wheel were no longer by the gate. I looked left and right to make sure I wasn't mistaken. Yep, they for sure weren't there. And then it happened. A big dough-like ball filled my throat and hot tears welled up in my eyes. Someone had taken my Big Wheel (never mind the missing couch and dresser). I immediately ran in the house yelling for my mom. She would find it. Mom knew where everything was.

In bursts of sobs and words, I was able to tell her about my powder puff. Mom's eyes shut for a second and her she hung her head down a bit. She already knew what had happened. Earlier in the day, my mom had called a local thrift store to come and pick up the couch and dresser. When she called me in for lunch, she didn't think that about where I would park my powder puff. While I was obliviously eating my tuna sandwich, the thrift store truck pulled up to our house and loaded the couch, the dresser, and my beloved bike in the back of the truck. They drove away taking a part of my childhood with them.

My mom tried to make the situation better. For the rest of the afternoon, we visited the local thrift stores trying to find my bike. She explained the situation, and management tried to be helpful, but the bike was already gone. Some other little girl was running her fingers through my handlebar tassels.

That is my first real memory of disappointment. Disappointment has become a theme throughout seasons of my life. Some of the disappointments in life are trivial and some are life changing.

The missing Big Wheel was trivial compared to the mystery lump on my neck.

My journey home from the doctor's office that afternoon, was not filled with elation, but instead an intense feeling of bewilderment. I was left wondering how the biopsy would affect the baby. To be honest, I didn't even really understand fully what having the biopsy entailed or why I even needed it so urgently. The news of "pink" was bullied to the side. The biopsy took center stage.

Jeff and I talked about the procedure and through the cracks in our voices, we did our best to think positively. Sometimes denial serves a purpose.

Two days later, I found myself in a hospital gown getting ready to go under the knife. Because of the length of the procedure, they needed to put me under general anesthesia. Again, I had questions of how the surgery would affect the baby. The doctor assured me that the baby would be safe. As they gave me the medicine to put me to sleep, I wondered if the baby would also be put to sleep. It's funny the things you think about before a surgery. "99, 98, 97.." I counted backwards not realizing I was forever saying goodbye to the "normal" life that I knew. While I was asleep, my whole universe was crumbling around me.

"Trina, can you hear me?" the nurse gently shook my hand. Bright lights. The sensation of vertigo. Eyes starting to open. Groggily, I climbed my way out of sedation. My senses started communicating with my brain—head pounding, fuzzy sight, confusion. The fuzzy realization that I was in the hospital. The sound of the rhythmic beep of the machine to my left. The nurse kept faintly calling me

by name. "Trina, wake up. You're out of surgery."
Coming back into reality was like pieces of a puzzle
slowly being put into place.

The nurse squeezed my hand and I looked
around for a familiar face. She told me that I was in
the recovery room and soon I would see my family.
It didn't take long for me to realize that I was starving. I couldn't wait to have a glass of water, some
Jell-O, toast, something to fill my belly. I wanted to
beg the nurse to bring me something, but when I
opened my mouth to talk a raspy, Phyllis Diller-
sounding voice painfully inched its way out of my
mouth. Unbeknownst to me, they intubated me
during the surgery, so that machines could breathe
for my body. I could hardly talk, but when the
nurse leaned over my bed, I found a way to whis-
per-beg for a sandwich.

The nurse left me alone in the room and a
few minutes later the doctor came in to give me an
update. He entered the room with a serious expression on his face. All of a sudden the climate
changed. He walked over to my bedside and
looked at me with regret in his eyes. He reached out
and held my hand. There's something so powerful
about human touch. Holding my hand communi-

cated to me that in that moment I was not alone. The doctor said "The surgery went well, but unfortunately, I have some bad news for you. You have Lymphoma."

Wait, what?

I had no idea what Lymphoma was, so I just shook my head and told him that was okay. I wanted him to think that I was brave. He clearly understood that I didn't know what he was talking about, so he tried to bring some clarity. "You have a form of Hodgkin's Disease." Now that sounded more serious, but to be honest with you, I didn't know what that was either. I thought about it for a minute, and then I shook my head and said I understood. *All I need are some antibiotics and my discharge papers.* Again, he knew that I didn't have a clue, so he decided to say it in terms that I could understand. And that's when he said the three words: "You have cancer."

Those three words stopped time and split history. Instantly my body went into shock. He kept talking, but I had no idea what he was saying. I wasn't even sure that he was talking to me; except the fact that he was looking right at me. I was 23 years old and facing the diagnosis of cancer. I had to work extra hard to focus on being present. In my mind, yesterday spilled into tomorrow. Everything was a mess. He kept talking, but the only two things that I remember was that I couldn't hear his voice, and tears kept falling off of my cheeks— though I didn't feel like I was crying. My body knew what my mind wasn't ready to comprehend, my life as I knew it, was over. I looked around the room for some escape or someone to tell him that he was wrong. That's when I realized that my family was not in the room. I was hearing this news alone. I was just numbly sitting there, holding hands with the doctor. He allowed time for me to process the news, although all I was doing was falling deeper into shock.

Hearing the news of having cancer changed everything. Before I was diagnosed, I was working overtime to make sure that my life was "perfect." My expectations were that if I were doing everything right, I wouldn't have any major struggles along the way. Naïve, I know. After hearing about the cancer, all I wanted to do was live.

Things moved pretty fast from the moment that I was diagnosed. When the doctor left the room, I was alone with the medical equipment and the monster called cancer that sucked all the air out of the room. I ached to see my husband. I truly believed that Jeff would make sense out of this, he would tell the doctors that they had made a horrible mistake. Denial was the cushion that kept me safe.

When I did see Jeff, he didn't walk in as a superhero vowing to save the day. He wore the same expression on his face that I was feeling in my heart—we were afraid.

Even in the surreal state of fear and denial, life moved forward. I was catapulted into a series of tests, CT scans, blood work, appointments, and specialists. Word traveled pretty fast through the medical community and I began to feel like I was wearing a cardboard sign around my neck that said, "Yes, I have cancer and I'm pregnant." Doctors would greet me with an apologetic tone in their voices. They knew the situation was much more serious than I did.

The first visit with my oncologist, a petite redheaded woman, gave me a much greater picture of the seriousness of cancer. I walked in to her office and emphatically stated that I would not be taking any chemotherapy until after the baby was born. In my mind, I could "tough it out." Dr. Petite sat back in her chair and said to me, "Trina, I hate to tell you this, but if you wait until the baby's born, there is a good chance that you will both die." The walls began to start inching their way across the room, closing in on me. My shirt felt like a turtleneck with its threads tightening around my neck. I shook my head, grasping for some sense of what she just said.

"What do you mean die?" I asked in disbelief. "Petite" explained to me that aside from the lump in my neck, common symptoms of the cancer were nausea and fatigue. Because I was experiencing the same symptoms with being pregnant, the cancer continued to spread throughout my body. What started in my neck had moved to my chest, then to my stomach. The last stop would be the bone marrow. Luckily, tests revealed that the marrow was clean, so it was imperative that I start treatment as soon as possible.

I was trying to process everything that she was saying. She sounded like she was mumbling into a tin can. I heard about 70% and comprehended about 30%. I was so glad that Jeff was with me to listen, gather information, and ask questions. Jeff started asking the questions that I could not think of. What type of treatment would I have to endure? How would chemotherapy impact the baby? Were there any other options?

Disconnected words floated like bubbles in the air. I'm not sure what context or order they belonged, I just heard them as singular words: uncertain, deformities, retardation, health, induction. Trying to grasp the concept of each word was like allowing bubbles of uncertainty to pop all over the place. The whole situation was a mess. The final recommendation was to get started immediately in order to give myself and the baby the best chance possible.

I left the office feeling disappointed, confused, and discouraged. I realized for the first time that I had little control over the circumstances I faced. As I made my way out to the car, I felt a slight fluttering in my belly. My Kate was talking to me, letting me know that she was there. This sweet little baby inside of me was telling me that we were in this together. I placed my hand on my belly and promised her that I would fight with all my heart. I would fight this cancer for both of us.

I started to feel heartbreak on a very deep level. It permeated every part of my being. I was disappointed with the cancer for existing. I was disappointed with my body for failing. I was disappointed in God for allowing it to happen. Being disappointed with God seemed wrong and foreign, but deep down, it was how I felt.

Suddenly, the verses that I had memorized in Sunday School took on a whole new meaning for me. For instance, Jeremiah 29:11: *"For I know the plans that I have for you. Plans to prosper and not to harm you. Plans to give you hope and a future."* I used to recite that verse with the certainty that it meant life would be prosperous and wonderful. Don't we always read that verse focusing on the hope and future?

My heart filtered this verse through a completely different life lens. *Was the cancer a part of God's plan? How would this bring me hope and a future?*

Day in and day out, I struggled with these types of questions on an emotional and spiritual level. The disappointment from the diagnosis of cancer was shattering everything I knew to be true.

I had to start back at square one in my beliefs.

And that's what I did. I started at square one. For the first time in my spiritual life, I started to ask the tough questions about faith. *Did God really exist? Did He hear my prayers? Did He see what I was going through? Did He even care?*

After numerous tests and appointments, it was decided that I would start my chemotherapy treatments while pregnant. They would treat me at my pre-pregnancy weight. The plan was to get the baby as far along as possible while I was doing chemotherapy, take a short break to have the baby, and to continue my treatment with aggressive chemotherapy after she was born. I didn't like the plan, but my options were limited.

My first chemotherapy appointment arrived much sooner than I anticipated. Walking into the building felt like I was giving in to the disease. Keeping the appointment made everything so real. I'm sure that every person feels misplaced and strange on his or her first treatment day, but I didn't just feel that way, I *looked* that way. The chemo room was filled with Lazy-Boy chairs lined up against the wall. At the end of the room, was a small television

showing a couple of perky day show hosts report-
ing the best way to make a summer quiche. So trivial.

People of all ethnicities, ages, and shapes
filled the chairs; their arms outstretched before
them with needles attached pumping them full of
the poisonous, but also potentially life-saving
chemotherapy. It's interesting how chemotherapy
can kill and heal at the same time. Cancer doesn't
discriminate. I looked at each person and wondered
about their story. Of course, they were all looking at
me. As I waddled down the aisle, all eyes fell directly to my protruding belly, then up to my eyes,
where I could see what they were feeling for me.
Despair.

The room was full, so the nurse led me to the
overflow. You know there is too much cancer in the
world when there are overflow rooms for chemotherapy. Actually, I didn't mind; a little more priva-
cy felt nice. The overflow room consisted of two
comfy recliners. To my left was an older woman
who could be a double for Angela Lansbury. She
was attached to her poison bag, quilt over her lap,
doing a crossword puzzle to pass time.

She looked up at me. Her eyes were kind, the color as deep as brown sugar. She had soft cheekbones and pale lips. I sheepishly looked at her and gave a polite nod. She looked at my belly, then my eyes, and in a gentle tone, said hello. The nurse showed me to my seat and then told me to get comfy. She brought me a blanket and a few magazines. Surely a stack of *People* magazines could make any situation better. She told me that she would return with an IV kit. I looked around thinking, *so this is where it all goes down*. Though the air was heavy, the room had a somewhat homey feel; serene paintings on the wall, positive quotes framed and placed on the counter, an endless row of paperback books. If I didn't know where I was, I would think I was in a retirement home.

The nurse returned with the IV kit. She sat down next to me and asked me a few questions about my situation. I think she was trying to distract me more than anything. Slight fist, quick poke, and she slid the needle into my vein. She whipped her tape out with her right hand and secured the needle in place. The first bag of my treatment was hung on the pole. She assured me that this was not the chemotherapy; it was the Heparin to clear my veins.

I started to do some crazy combination of internal positive self-talk and desperate praying. The Heparin dripped through the tube and into my veins. Not so bad. After all, it wasn't the chemotherapy. I felt Kate kick within my belly, reminding me that we were in this together. *I can do this. I can do this.* Within a few minutes the bag of Heparin was empty. Like clockwork, the nurse returned to the room with another bag full of liquid. She removed the first bag and connected the second. "This is your first treatment of chemotherapy, Trina. I will be back in every few minutes to check on you." She patted my hand, adjusted the settings on my pump, and left the room.

I panicked. What was I doing? This was insane. Didn't they know that I was pregnant? How could I even take the chemotherapy? What kind of mom would do that to her baby? I want out. Now! My heart started to race. I felt like a trapped animal. I didn't want to do it anymore; any of it. I wanted desperately to go back four weeks to when my life was normal. I wanted to fast forward five months and hold my healthy baby. I wanted to be anywhere but sitting in that room. I was trying to remain so brave on the outside, but my emotions spilled out of my eyes. Hot tears slid down my cheeks and landed on my shirt. I was resigned to my situation. There was nothing that I could do. I was a pregnant woman taking her first chemotherapy. Shame and fear swirled around in my head. Shame because I felt like I was failing my daughter, fear because I couldn't control the future.

Though I tried to keep a controlled poker face, the tears and look of terror gave me away. The woman in the recliner next to me looked my way. She gently reached over and held my hand. She looked me straight in the eyes and said, "It's okay, Sweetie. Everyone cries the first time. You *are* going to be okay." And that was it. She squeezed my hand, let go, and went back to solving her cross-word puzzle. As soon as she spoke those words, something profound happened. A peace that I cannot describe comforted me like a warm blanket. The air became breathable and my anxiety started to dissolve.

Her words breathed peace in my heart.

God used this woman to speak life to me. In that moment, it was undeniable that God was there with me in that room. I passed the time praying, reading, and wondering about the future. I finished my chemotherapy treatment that day with a renewed perspective. I didn't know what the future held, but I knew I wasn't alone.

I walked away emotionally and physically exhausted. Life had been an incredible whirlwind. But, for the first time since the diagnosis, I felt something stirring in the depth of my soul. An overwhelming feeling was bubbling up from within. It reached my heart and mind at the same time. My mouth opened and I called it out by name, hope.

Chapter Three: Hamburger Helper and Half-Marathons

"In everyone's life, at some time, our inner fire goes out. It is then burst into flame by an encounter with another human being. We should all be thankful for those people who rekindle the inner spirit." Albert Schweitzer

Expectations have a powerful influence on my attitudes and actions. Recently I opened a letter that I had written to my future self when I was a senior in high school. The letter was filled with questions about my life as an adult. Was I married? Did I have a career? How many children did I have? I had so many expectations about how my life would and should turn out. Life and relationships don't always unfold the way we plan. I think that marriage really made me realize how many expectations that I had in place for relationship, and how my expectations shaped my early years together with Jeff.

From the moment I met Jeff, I knew there was something different about him. He had kind eyes and a gentle soul. He was an introvert with an adventurous spirit. I found him incredibly attractive. Jeff and I had an incredibly romantic dating life; late nights in coffee shops, long drives by the ocean, dinners and movies. We lived in San Francisco, the perfect city for romance.

The romance factor changed when we got married. We settled into life together pretty quickly. All of the hidden "ugliness" crept out. He didn't lower the toilet seat after he used the bathroom and he claimed that I had the worst morning breath, jury is still out on that one.

My expectation was that marriage would

come easy to us, as easy as dating. But the reality is, we were combining two lives into one, there are going to be unexpected hiccups along the way. I remember one of my biggest complaints in marriage was that Jeff was no longer as romantic as he once was while we were dating. One night we were watching a movie that changed everything. The brawny man on the television screen gently reached over and took his date by the arm, he gave her a playful flick of the wrist. She looked at him lovingly, knowing what she was about to do. In slow motion, she rolled into his arms. He dipped her at the waist, looked into her eyes, and said "Kiss me, you fool."

I enthusiastically piped in, "Jeff, this is what I'm talking about. This is the type of romance that I am missing." Jeff looked at me, almost confused. "You mean you want me to dip you?" He was totally missing the point. I didn't want him to dip me, I wanted him to have the attitude of romanticism in everything that we did. I was so idealistic.

Trying to please me, Jeff filed my request away. A few days later, I was in the kitchen making Hamburger Helper (my specialty), when Jeff reached over and gently put his hand around my wrist. He had a playful look in his eye as he gave my wrist and little tug. I knew exactly what he was doing, so I played my part perfectly. With my toes barely touching the floor, twirled into his arms. He dipped me at the waist, looked lovingly into my eyes, and said, "Kiss me, stupid." One word can change the meaning of a whole gesture.

By the look on my face, he could tell that he had done something wrong, although he didn't know what. "Stupid" and "You fool" are not synonymous. The truth is that in those days, my expectations far outweighed the grace that I was willing to extend. From his point of view, he was trying to do exactly what I wanted, to become a little more romantic. I was the one who was shortsighted and who missed a chance to laugh at our silly "romantic" moment.

The same attitude of expectations that let me down in the kitchen tortured me during my cancer. I wanted the journey to be my way, on my terms. If I was going to be sick, dang it, I was still going to be in control. Or so I thought.

Nothing went the way I had planned. Not the pregnancy, the treatment, or the disease that was assaulting my body. But in the same breath, I found tremendous gifts in the things that didn't go my way. My prayers started to change. They became very raw and real. For the first time I was truly crying out to God. Scripture started to come alive. The verses that spoke of hope and healing were especially vibrant to me. I started to understand *community* for the first time. Friends showed up in moments when I needed them most, and sometimes when I was too proud to ask for help.

Before I was sick, I prided myself on being a person who helped others. If someone needed a meal after a baby was born, I would sign up. If someone wanted a few hours of childcare to do a solo shopping trip, I was always willing to step in. Need someone to come in and help set up the tables? Count on Trina. There's nothing wrong with wanting to help people, but I had a different problem buried deep within my heart. I didn't want to receive.

After the diagnosis and the initial chemotherapy treatments, I was utterly exhausted. I was so focused on getting healthy that I didn't have time to focus on the normal duties of life. I can't tell you how many times the doorbell rang with a friend holding a meal. I was humbled by the numerous phone calls of people encouraging me and asking how they could help. Friends showing up to help clean, watch my kids, and just sit and be with me. It was incredibly humbling and I was very uncomfortable with all of the help. Something in me wanted to prove that I could do it alone, that I didn't need all the help and charity. But the truth was that I was very sick and I had a toddler running around. I *did* need the help, I was just too proud to admit it. And that's how I learned that pride was hurting me. Pride kept me from building real relationships. Pride talked me out of being candid for fear of looking weak. Pride kept me from saying the words, that I knew were true: "I need help."

The interesting thing about having cancer while I was pregnant is that I couldn't hide my pain. Everyone knew I was sick, everyone knew I was hurting, and everyone knew I needed help. But even when help was offered I had to have a spirit of humility to accept it.

I had to learn the hard way that we are not meant to suffer through life's battles alone.

We have all had expectations that have let us

down. The mother who suffers with post-partum depression never imagined that days after giving birth to her child, she would feel so disconnected and down, yet she suffers alone. The woman who is in a marriage that is cracking around her doesn't share with anyone for fear of being judged. Instead she suffers alone. The family who is working like crazy to make ends meet and struggling with fore-closure doesn't share their financial struggles for fear of embarrassment and shame. They suffer alone. We are not meant to suffer alone, we are meant to journey with each other along the way.

—

In my early thirties, I decided to run a half marathon. I'm not a runner, but I did expect that running would come easy to me. How hard could it really be? Buy some new sneakers, stretch a little, and start running. Voila!

As soon as I signed up, I decided to drive the entire distance of the run, just to get a feel for the adventure ahead of me. I was about three miles into the drive when I realized that I had made a huge mistake, 13.1 miles is a long way to drive! All of the sudden, running that distance seemed impossible, but I had made the commitment and I was determined.

My friends stepped in to help. My friend Kim is a runner and she signed on for training with me. My friends Sharon and Corinne decided to train from afar and meet with me on race day. Instantly, I had a community around me. Kim and I would meet up on the weekends for long runs. The first couple of runs were really tough, and I didn't think that I would be able to continue. My legs ached like crazy after each run. I was tired, awkward, and clearly out of shape. Time after time, Kim would show up at my door for a run. It didn't take too long before my body started to respond. Running got a little easier when I learned how to find my own rhythm.

In order to prepare for the big race, Kim suggested that we sign up for a local 10K. It would be an official introduction to the competitive running world. I am a realist. I wasn't shooting to win the race; the name of the game was finishing with the best time possible.

Kim and I paid our entrance fees, pinned our numbers to our shirts, and lined up at the start line. There was so much energy and excitement in the air. When the race started we were running with a large group of people, but within the first mile, the pack thinned out. Some were slower, most were faster. I was more comfortable with the slower. The first three miles were pretty easy, but starting the fourth, I started to get tired. The excitement had long since left me. I still had three miles to go. We reached the turnaround mark and started on our way back. I slowed quite a bit and told Kim that I wanted to walk. She stuck with me, walking when I needed to. Step by step, we kept going. Just when I didn't think I could make it to the finish line, Kim pulled her earbuds out and said, "Trina, the finish line is really close, if you have to catch your breath, do it now. You're going to want to run over that finish line." There couldn't have been sweeter words to hear. We were close. I was actually going to finish this 10K!

I drew fresh breath and with renewed hope, picked up my pace. The closer I got to the finish line, the more I heard the crowd cheer. Then I saw it, the actual finish line. I picked up my pace, held my head up high, and smiled from ear-to-ear as I crossed that finish line. The feeling of accomplishment was deep within my soul. The girl who never got picked for sports in grade school, who was cut from the basketball team, had finished the race. I didn't do it alone. Kim was there the whole run, cheering me on, every step of the way. That's when it occurred to me that Kim could have run that 10K much faster by herself. Instead, she paid her entrance fee and ran at my pace. Her time didn't matter, the journey of finishing together did. True friendship has incredible marks of sacrifice. Her gesture was a reminder of the importance of friendship. The importance of community. And the importance of journeying the road of life together.

———

I live in one of the most beautiful places in the world, where the redwood trees meet the ocean. It's a quaint little county at the top of California. Humboldt County is off the beaten path, but if you ever venture this way, I assure you that you will see a glimpse of God's beauty and grandeur. The redwood trees are a constant reminder to me that life is much bigger and grandiose. As beautiful as the trees are, there is a more powerful meaning hidden in the roots of a redwood.

Redwood trees can exceed over 300 feet in height. Yet these gentle giants that soar so high into the heavens, have a relatively shallow root system. So how do they stay upright?

The roots of a redwood only grow four to six feet deep and about 125 feet wide. That doesn't provide a lot of support for such a large tree. Wind, rain, and erosion can easily compromise the root system causing the tree to fall over. How do the trees stand up? The roots of the redwood tree frequently grow intertwined with the roots of other redwoods. By being intertwined underground, they form a network that provides the strength needed to stand.

I see these trees as a perfect illustration of how we should function in community. Through the great storms of life we should "hold hands" and hold each other up.

Two are better than one,
because they have a good return for their work:

If either of them falls down,
one can help the other up.
But pity anyone who falls
and has no one to help them up.
Ecclesiastes 4:9-10

We are meant for relationships: sharing stories, laughter, faith, and life. It's in our conversations and prayers. Showing up. Listening. Being available. Going through the grit of life together. Being transparent, and at times, being broken. It's healing and hopeful. Forgiving and being forgiven.

In the most difficult situations in life, we are reminded that we need to "hold hands" in the stormy weather.

That's what friendship looks like. It's the people who will stand beside you when it gets tough. It's the people who believe in you when you are trying something new. It's the people who will run at "your pace" and encourage you along the way. We all need this type of community around us.

Our expectation should be that life can be tough and unpredictable. Whatever comes our way, it's important that we journey together with friends. We don't need to have it all together all of the time. There is freedom in being transparent, sharing our burdens, and accepting help when we need it. This is how we will build true community.

Chapter Four: Stranger in the Starbucks Drive-Thru

"We're one, but we're not the same. We get to carry each other, carry each other." One- U2

When Caleb was a toddler he loved reaching out of the grocery cart and putting goodies in the basket. In one instance, he took dishwashing detergent off of the shelf when I wasn't looking. He opened the cap, turned the bottle upside down, and let the soap drip steadily as we walked through the market. Perhaps he thought of himself as a young Picasso painting on an oversized canvas.

I didn't realize that he was "drawing on the ground" until I felt my shoe give a little. I looked down and saw the blue soap on the shiny floor. My eyes followed the trail of liquid that ran down the entire aisle, then I looked at my son. He grinned and held the bottle up for me to see. The soap trail must have been at least four aisles long. My heart went out to the teenage stock boy who had to clean it up. Embarrassed and overwhelmed, I took my son home with my pre-children refrain of "my kid would never…" ringing in my ears.

Another time, I was shopping with Caleb and he kept trying to climb out of the shopping cart. This began another saga of me trying to hold him with one hand, shop with the other hand, and push the cart with my stomach. These days, I see moms do all of that while holding a Starbucks and talking on their cell phones. That takes "super-mom" to another dimension. I was trying to keep Caleb in the cart, while shopping, and doing both unsuccessfully. From the other side of the aisle, I saw an older woman looking my way. Instantly, I felt insecure about my parenting abilities. I was sure that she was judging my inability to control my child.

Caleb continued to climb out of the cart with renewed energy. As my panic to control him grew, the woman continued to glance my way. Slowly she started walking toward me. *I knew it. She's gonna tell me that I'm a bad mom.* The woman walked up to my cart and said, "You know, when my kids were little they wouldn't sit in the cart. They would do just like your son and try to climb out at every opportunity. A great way to fix that problem is to tie his shoelaces together. He won't be able to get out." Then she smiled and turned around and walked away.

I laughed out loud. Genius! She was no longer the woman judging me, she became the fellow mother, an unexpected mentor sharing her wisdom with a younger (and less experienced) mom. Her kindness was a gift.

That's the best word I can use to describe kindness—a gift. We all need the gift of kindness in our lives. Kindness is the action that tells us that we are valued, cared for, and loved. Sometimes kindness shows up in small ways—as in a grocery store, and sometimes kindness shows up in a big way—as in a life crisis. I've been on the receiving end of both.

For me, one of the life's greatest crises was taking chemotherapy while pregnant. The reality of chemotherapy was sobering. The cocktail was essentially poisoning the good and bad cells in my body. The question always lingered, if this chemotherapy is so toxic that it can make my hair fall out, what does that mean for my unborn child? Science can only tell you so much. Unfortunately, the rest was played out in my imagination.

As I walked into the chemotherapy room for each treatment, I willed myself to each step. I couldn't digest the whole scenario, or even the task for that day, I only willed myself *one* step at a time. The procedure became familiar; needle inserted into vein, bag hanging from pole, blanket on my lap, and the four-hour countdown until I was finished.

Those four hours in the chair gave me way too much time to think, to worry. Too much time allowed my mind to wander the dark hallways of possibility. Thankfully, my friends made sure that I didn't spend all of my treatments alone. They would show up to visit, play cards, and just chat. I needed the interaction and distraction—and they knew it.

After my treatments, I always felt like I had been hit by a semi-truck. All I wanted to do was to go home and sleep. The word "tired" doesn't really describe the actual feeling. It's more than tired. It's weary, broken, tired, fatigued, spent, and drained all rolled into one. Of course, I don't know how much of that was having cancer, being pregnant, or the combination of both. All I knew was that my body was hitting capacity and I wasn't sure how much more I was able to take.

As the weeks passed, my body started to change. My hair thinned, my eyes became dark and tired, my skin was dry and flaky, and my lips lacked their normal pink tint. I looked closer to death than life. On days I cared to try, I would fake it with makeup. But even as my face was showing the effects of the chemotherapy, my body continued to grow with new life.

My doctor wanted to deliver Kate as soon as her lungs were developed. She had already gone through four treatments of chemotherapy and as far as we could tell, she was doing okay. At the thirty-six week mark, they decided to schedule the induction date, pending amniocentesis results showing that her lungs were developed.

I was riding an emotional roller coaster. In the middle of the greatest heartache of my life, I was about to meet my daughter. I felt like I was experiencing a glimpse of blue sky in the midst of a storm. Kate's delivery would be the moment when joy would shine out of brokenness. It was the hope moment that kept me going. I longed to see the face of my daughter; to know that she was okay.

A few days before my induction date, I arrived at my doctor's office for my weekly visit. I was led into a room where my doctor looked over my chart, checked my vitals, and asked how I was feeling. It was an unusually brief appointment. When I was being led out of the room, he asked me to follow him to the back. He opened the door to the staff break room and to my surprise it was filled with all of the nurses. Presents were on the tables, pink balloons and streamers hung from the ceiling and there was a cake with Kate's name on it. The nurses had surprised me with a baby shower.

I was stunned. The nurses and doctors—who were doing the best they could to save my life—took time out of their day to meet my needs in a different way. They knew how hard the whole experience had been for me. In the thick of medication, chemotherapy, surgery, and endless appointments, they joined in the celebration of Kate's birth.

I was completely humbled. More than the gifts and the cake, I was humbled by the kindness and generosity shown to me on that day. I felt undeserving of such extravagant care.

My life during that time was an unusual paradox. My body was breaking down physically, but my spirit was being renewed by the kindness and love of others. I was experiencing God's goodness through people.

But as much as I was experiencing kindness in my sickness, I was also learning another valuable life lesson; kindness is not shown to everyone. The same time that I was struggling through my cancer, I had a friend that was struggling through alcoholism. She was lonely, hurt, depressed, and addicted. She often felt judged and ostracized. We both were experiencing pain, just in different ways.

People were constantly around me asking what they could do to help. My friend didn't have much support at all. She was left alone to deal with her pain.

It was in those moments that I started to realize that sometimes we show kindness and love to the people that we think deserve it, forgetting about those on the margins. We decide who is and who isn't worthy of care. I know, because I was the greatest offender. I realized that in my own life, I had withheld kindness and generosity from people that I didn't think "deserved" it. It wasn't something that I consciously did, it was more of a heart attitude. I needed to have a heart change about the ways that I would show kindness and love- even when I didn't understand the pain of other people.

A couple of years ago, I was able to see my favorite band in concert. Seeing U2 perform was probably one of the most powerful experiences that I've ever had. As I entered the stadium, I was overwhelmed by the size of the stage and the number of people in attendance. With almost 70,000 people, it seemed like standing in the middle of a small city.

As the band came on the stage and started playing their songs. I looked around the stadium and I thought to myself, these people are all from different walks of life, different lifestyles, different cultures, and different political parties. We are all so different, but we have one thing in common. We *all* love this band.

For a moment I got a glimpse of what community is supposed to look like. It's *supposed* to be full of people who have differences, but yet who are united by the love that they have for each other.

True community includes everyone: the stay-at-home mom, the professional, the alcoholic, the missionary, the liberal, the pregnant teen, the single mom, the conservative, the activist, the prisoner, and the rock star. It includes me. It's all of us.

And we are all very different. We need to learn how to celebrate our difference and show kindness to one another. Our diversity is a gift from God.

The picture of the stadium will stay with me for a long time. Though we were 70,000 individuals, when the music started to play, we became one community.

In true community we should care for each other. Every day we come in contact with people who are hurting and overwhelmed. We have no idea what an act of kindness will mean in their day. It can be as simple as a smile or a sweet word of encouragement.

A few days ago, I was racing to get some errands done. I decided to stop into Starbucks for a quick pick-me-up. As I pulled in the drive thru, another car pulled up at the same time. Honestly, she did get there before me—even if it was just by inches. I waved at her to go through. She smiled and I waved back. The line was longer than usual, but it was a nice break in the rush. When I pulled up to the window, the barista told me that my drinks had been paid for, then she handed me this note.

"Thanks for letting me in ahead of you. Spent most of the day in the E.R. with my mom. On the way to pick her up and take her home. Even small acts of kindness can mean a lot."

I had no clue, how could I have? All I did

was wave her through, but she gave me the greatest gift of all; the perspective that the things that I do and say make a difference in the lives of others. Sometimes it's in the big gestures, but more often it's in the small, unnoticed moments. Kindness can change everything.

Chapter Five: Welcome to Life

"When we are no longer able to change a situation - we are challenged to change ourselves." Viktor E. Frankl

In August 2010, 33 men found themselves trapped in a Chilean mine 2,300 feet underground. Those 33 men clocked in that morning, anticipating a normal workday. How could they have known that hours later, their lives would be changed forever?

The whole world watched as the events of the Chilean mining accident started to unfold. An unexpected cave-in, blinding dust, and no escape route. The future looked bleak. In response to their situation, the 33 men started to organize themselves into a daily routine—waiting for rescue. Sixty-nine days after the cave-in a large drill finally broke through to the miners and created a shaft that would allow them to be rescued. Over the course of 24 hours, one-by-one, each miner was lifted to the surface. Can you imagine how their perspective had changed? From being a hard working miner, trapped under the earth for two months, then lifted to freedom. As one of the miners was being pulled from the shaft, Chilean President Sebastian Pinera leaned over and said to the miner, "Welcome to life."

Welcome to life. We've all been there, in some way. It's the moment when you don't think that life could get worse, then all of the sudden, something changes, and it's a "Welcome to life" moment.

The truth is that adversity and unexpected struggles do change us in a profound way. Because of those experiences, we see life through a new lens. I'm sure the Chilean miners appreciated the fresh air in a new way. The same fresh air that we breath every day ... and we don't even realize how fortunate we are. That is the power of perspective.

On July 29, 2000, I got to have a "Welcome to life" moment ... literally. Through all of the heartache, chemotherapy, and discouragement, I was ready to meet my daughter. Kate had already endured four treatments of chemotherapy in utero and though she was six weeks early, the doctors found it best to induce my labor. Being induced six weeks early was essentially asking my body to perform a task it wasn't ready for.

I was dealing with so many emotions. I was going to see my baby girl, but I was so nervous about how she had been affected by the chemotherapy. We arrived at the hospital at our appointed time, filled out the paperwork, and found ourselves in a deluxe maternity room and the end of the hall. The staff was well aware of our special circumstances and did everything that they could to make sure that I was comfortable. After checking my vitals and giving me an IV, the nurse started my pitocin. My sweet MOPS friends filled my room with balloons and flowers. We sat around talking and laughing. It was a day to celebrate. So we waited. And waited. It didn't seem like much was happening.

After my family and friends left from an uneventful day, I went to bed that evening feeling discouraged at my lack of progress. Jeff knew that I was discouraged. He reached over from his makeshift bed and held my hand as I drifted to sleep. In the middle of the night, my body started to respond to the pitocin. The pain was instantly excruciating. The labor was intense and progressed quickly. Eleven minutes after my water broke, my daughter made her entrance into the world. Kate was small, but healthy. She weighed in at 4 lbs. 8 oz. The sound of her cry was that of a small warrior. She was a fighter.

When I saw her little face, fingers, toes, healthy pink skin—I knew that she was going to be okay. In the midst of my own life health crisis, she was the most beautiful sight on earth. Her birth was a "Welcome to life" for both of us. She was the beauty in the midst of my broken body.

From my perspective, the hardest part of the cancer up to that point was taking the chemotherapy and not knowing the long-term effects it would have on Kate. No one could tell for sure how she would be affected. In the moments following her delivery and hearing her sweet cries, I knew the greater half of my battle was over. The mama-bear in me knew that once I saw that my baby was okay, the doctors could do whatever they wanted to me.

The doctors whisked Kate away to check her vitals and make sure that she was completely healthy. I didn't get experience the moments of having her in my room with me, showing her off to family and friends. Because of her circumstances, Kate needed to be in the NICU for observation. Jeff and I sat next to her little plastic crib. We talked to Kate and assured her that we were there. We held her little hands and feet. And when it was time to leave, I put her little plush pink giraffe close to her body for comfort. The hardest part of her being in the NICU was knowing that I couldn't be with her the whole time. We would have to walk back to my room if I wanted rest. It was heartbreaking to sit on my hospital bed and hear the babies crying in the room next door.

Caleb wanted to meet his new sister. The hospital had strict rules about people who were allowed to enter the NICU and because of his age,

Caleb did not meet the requirements. I am forever grateful to the nurse who found a way to make their first introduction happen. My mom stood outside the unit doors and held Caleb up to the windows. The nurse rolled Kate, along with all of her attachments, to the doors so that my son could meet his baby sister for the first time. It was a very sweet moment.

As much as Kate fought in the womb, she too worked at adjusting to her new surroundings. Unfortunately, she wouldn't stay awake long enough to drink her milk. Because of her special circumstances, and her inability to stay awake long enough to eat, she had to stay in the NICU for 3 ½ weeks. Three days after delivering her, I was discharged from the hospital. I walked into the hospital with Kate in my belly, and I was leaving the hospital without her. Though it was the best care for Kate, it felt totally unnatural to be separated from my daughter.

My body was given a nine day rest before I started my new, more aggressive treatment. In those nine days, I tried to adjust to my new normal. Sometimes I would think, *"How in the world did I make it through that?"* I had all the "normal" post-partum feelings, regular visits to Kate in the NICU, taking care of my Caleb, visiting my OBG/YN and going to appointments with my oncologist. Plus I was facing chemotherapy and the painful process of drying up my chemotherapy-filled breast milk. *Side note: frozen cabbage leaves really do work. I smelled like an old coleslaw salad, but my milk quickly dried up.*

Those three weeks of having Kate in the NICU felt like a never-ending tornado, a whirlwind of appointments, emotions, and changes. Trying to find balance was like standing on a basketball, I couldn't do it for long. One day, I'd had enough. I was sick of being sick. I was totally frustrated that I couldn't take my daughter home. I was over-whelmed about losing my hair. I'd just plain had enough. I grabbed some Comet and a scrub brush and headed to the bathroom to clean the tub. You might be thinking that is an irrational response to stress, and it was.

I scrubbed and cried and scrubbed some more. Honestly, I think I scrubbed some of the lac-quer off of the tub. That tub was the recipient of my anger, frustration, and sorrow. In the middle of my fit, I looked up to find my mom standing in the doorway, her eyes filled with sympathy.

"What are you doing, hon?" she asked.

"I'm just scrubbing the tub, it needed to be cleaned." It was obvious that I had been crying. My face was swollen, red, and hot tears were still running down my face. My mom knew that I was at capacity and I let her have it. "I'm tired of this. I want my baby to come home from the hospital, my hair is falling out, I have so much more treatment that I still have to do." I laid into my mom and she took it like a trooper. She let me finish before she took a step closer. I knew that my mom couldn't fix any of it, she knew that too. It was probably harder for her to watch her child go through this than it was for me to walk the journey.

My mom took a step closer, leaned over and with a sympathetic voice, said, "Who wants a Frappuccino?" It was the best line ever and instantly I started laughing. The truth is that's all that she could do to momentarily relieve some of the pressure. And she did just that, we got into her minivan, and made our way to the closest Starbucks. For just a moment, my life felt a little normal. Just a mom and her daughter heading out for an afternoon treat.

In the grit of life, perspective becomes one of the most important tools of survival. When I was training for my half-marathon, I could not imagine the perspective that I would gain from the process of training and actually running (and walking) a half marathon. Part of what made the half marathon so special was that the route went right past the building where I took my chemotherapy.

On the morning of the run, my two friends and I got up early, put on our running gear, and headed down to the start line. Thousands of people lined the streets of San Diego. Everywhere I looked, runners were preparing for the challenge ahead of them. The energy in the air was electric. I joined my friends in the sea of runners. In that moment, I felt so connected to the experience. Aside from my friends, I didn't know anyone in the crowd, but I felt like we were a part of a community. We were all runners about to experience a challenge and we were going to do it together.

The sound of the gunshot echoed through the air and we took off. My friend Sharon ran up ahead as she had signed on for the full marathon. Corinne and I started our first two miles strong. We ran off of the cheers from the crowds on the sidelines. I felt great, accomplished, and inspired. I was a true runner. But as the spectators thinned out and the cheering stopped, I stared to realize that I had a long road ahead of me. Literally. Corinne was running strong, but adjusted her pace to compensate for mine. She also was kind enough to hold all of my granola bars and energy supplements in her runner's pack.

As we navigated through the city streets, I felt the burning in my legs and the ache in my knees. I became discouraged and started thinking about all of the reasons that I probably would not be able to finish the race. Corinne encouraged me to keep on. Step by step. We slowed to a jog, then to a walk. At that point we were about seven miles in. The electricity in the air was long gone. I was winded, sweaty, hungry, and spent. Winston Churchill once said, "If you're going through hell, keep going." I was in running hell and I was ready to throw in the towel. A lump formed in my throat as I told her that I didn't think I could continue. The beautiful thing about true friends is that they usually see strength in us that we don't see in ourselves. Corinne told me to keep going. Quitting wasn't an option.

I put my head down and willed myself to keep going all the while having a pity party inside. Then I heard a woman coming up from behind me. She was yelling to the runners ahead of her. "What mile are we at?" And that's when I saw her. She was a runner in her seemingly mid-sixties using a walking stick to tap out a clear path in front of her. I swallowed my pride and yelled out, "You're at marker mile 7". She thanked me and continued on her way. She was blind and running. She couldn't see the road in front of her, but she continued to run along without hesitation.

Seeing the blind runner instantly gave me perspective. I was a young woman, in good health, with perfect vision and I was just getting ready to "throw in the towel." What was I thinking? Running the half marathon was an opportunity for me to challenge myself, not wallow in self-pity. With the help of Corinne's encouragement and seeing the blind runner, I became determined to finish the race. Though my pace left a lot to be desired, I kept on. It wasn't too long before I saw the hospital on my left. That hospital represented a very difficult time in my life. It was the same hospital where I took my chemotherapy—the same hospital where I

was facing death. To think of sitting in that chemotherapy unit years before and the reality of running
by it were almost too much to comprehend.

As I passed the mile marker ten, then eleven,
I knew that I could finish the half marathon. My
body ached, and my muscles burned with lactic
acid, but I willed myself to keep going. The closer
we got to the finish line, the more people lined up
on the side cheering us on. Because a large group of
the runners (including myself) were running with
Team in Training, people on the sidelines held
posters up thanking us for our efforts. One sign
said, "thank you for running for my son," another
"my dad thanks you for running." Running to help
fund research for a cure was an incredibly humbling experience. It was through research that the
medical community was able to find a cure for
Hodgkin's Lymphoma. I felt like this run was my
small part to give back.

Up ahead in the distance, I finally saw it—the
finish line. The cheers from the crowds progressive-
ly got louder. My stride got better. Tears fell down
my cheeks. I was actually going to make it. I had
trained for six months for this moment. I crossed
the finish line and threw my arms up in the air.

Straight ahead of me was Jeff. I limp/walked over to him as fast as I could and fell into his arms, crying. The half marathon was about so much more than running. It was about challenging myself to complete something physically demanding. It was about joining a community of runners to help those fighting with cancer. It was about finding the perspective that life is sometimes like a marathon—even when it gets tough, we have to keep going.

———

One of the toughest moments during the cancer was losing my hair. It's not that I had great hair like Farrah Fawcett. My hair was simple, fine, and mousy-brown. It doesn't matter, really. The point is that it was MY hair.

Shortly after I delivered Kate, my hair started to fall out rapidly. First I noticed a strand or two, then ten, then clumps. I brushed it ever so carefully as not to encourage the loss. It didn't matter. All it took for the hair to fall was a slight shift of my head or a small gust of wind. It was inevitable. I was going bald.

I knew about the hair loss going into the

treatment, but there was no way that I could prepare myself for what it would feel like to watch it go. It was downright depressing. After days of watching the hair fall out, I announced to my husband. "That's it, we're shaving my head." Just saying the words filled me with a newfound sense of empowerment. *Ha! Take that cancer. You've ruined enough of my life. You can't take my hair. Only I get to make that choice.*

There was no stopping me. By that afternoon, I was sitting at my in-law's home. My brother-in-law so graciously stepped forward to do the honors. First, he cut my hair short, then he got the clippers out and shaved my head. I could see the hair fall over my nose and float to the floor. I recently watched the scene in *Les Miserables* where Anne Hathaway is having her hair chopped off. The scene instantly brought me back to that chair, in the family room, having my head shaved.

My poor husband didn't know how to respond or what to say. He just knew I "needed" to do it. With my clean-shaven head, I would no longer have to see the daily proof of the effects of the chemotherapy. I stood up, ran my hand over my shorn scalp, and smiled with renewed perspective.

Cancer didn't get to win the hair battle.

Chapter Six: Jesus in New York

You've got to get yourself together
You've got stuck in a moment
And you can't get out of it. -U2

I have a group of girlfriends with whom I travel every year. We've been to Nashville, Austin, Yosemite, Hawaii, Las Vegas, San Francisco, and most recently, New York. I had never been to New

York before, and to be honest, my mind was filled with stereotypes; rude people, pizza on every corner, overpriced food—you name it, I was ignorant about it. But nonetheless, I was excited to go to the Big Apple. Actually there was a specific reason for the New York trip. My friend Sharon was turning forty and her husband decided to surprise her by sending her friends on a trip to New York (we all thought Mark had an incredible idea!). Sharon had no idea that for months we had all been scheming together talking about what we would do, the places we would visit, and how we would surprise her.

Early on the morning of her birthday, our friend Corinne and I let ourselves into Sharon's house and climbed into a wrapped refrigerator box. The time came for Mark to wake Sharon up and lead her down the stairs. We heard some voices, then the sound of footsteps on the stairs. A tired Sharon stood in front of the box and said, "Is it going to pop out at me?" And we did pop out, somewhat out of excitement, but mostly out of the feeling of claustrophobia.

Sharon was surprised and confused. So confused, in fact, that she just stared at us and said,

"What is going on?"

Before she could even wrap her brain around what was happening, we whisked her up to her room to start packing. We were on our way to New York, with one stop in Missouri to pick up our other friend Jenn. Four friends in New York City for four days. Could it get any better?

We did it all, well as much as we could cram in. We went to the Top of the Rock, took the NBC Studio Tours, visited the Empire State Building, took a tour of Central Park, saw Jimmy Fallon live, watched *Mary Poppins* on Broadway, stood in Times Square, had cake from The Cake Boss's bakery (Thanks Armida), and spent time reflecting at the 9/11 Memorial.

Honestly, It was an overwhelming experience. And for the record, my stereotypes about New Yorkers were completely proven wrong. The people of New York City are incredible. They are friendly, helpful, and so proud of their city. I loved talking to the people in the city. I got to hear so many different perspectives of life in the city, and most of the conversations, sooner or later, would end up around 9/11. It was humbling to hear about where people were, what they experienced, the fear that they felt. If you ask anyone in the United States where they were on that Tuesday morning, they could answer you, because they remember. The beautiful people of New York didn't just remember 9/11 as images on the news, they lived it. It was their police force, their family members, and their city. Though it had been more than ten years since 9/11, I felt compelled to express my heartfelt condolences for what they had experienced, and still are experiencing. The people of New York are brave and resilient.

As I walked around the city, I was in awe of the different cultures, ethnicities, foods, and languages. New York is a beautiful kaleidoscope of diversity. And there is an unexplainable electricity in the air.

On one of our bus tours, we drove right past the Metropolitan Museum of Art, commonly referred to as The Met. I was so excited. The Met was right in front of me, the building that held thousands of incredible pieces of art. I wanted so badly to get off of the tour bus and see the art in The Met.

In order to complete my Bachelor's degree, I

was required to take an Art History class. I was not happy about having to take the class because I didn't think I was interested in art; actually, I had never been exposed to art. That art class ended up being one of my favorite classes of all time. I was able to study the different styles of art, the meaning behind the art, and the biographies of the artists themselves.

The deeper I got into studying the art, the more I realized the art was speaking to me. I loved looking at the paintings and surveying the meaning. I would read about the time in history when the art was created and question what the artist was trying to convey. What did the colors mean? The shapes? The tones? Every piece of art could be interpreted a thousand different ways.

In my art history class, we spent a significant amount of time studying the Sistine Chapel. This is where the art became personal to me. There is something very special and spiritual about the Sistine Chapel. It's not just because the paintings are about God and his relationship with man, that is special in and of itself. What I mean by special is that there is something much greater going on with the Sistine Chapel. The fact that Michelangelo painted the Sistine Chapel in four years is incredible, but what I find still more amazing, is that hundreds of years later, people from all over the world travel to Italy to line up and view the frescos in the Sistine Chapel. Men and women of all ages squeeze into the chapel look at the art, interpret the meaning, and to contemplate God. It is on my bucket list to one day squeeze into that chapel, look at the art, take in what God inspired and Michelangelo painted. How can one man's gift for painting impact so many people? A greater question for each of us is how can we use our gifts to do the same?

After our bus tour, we decided to backtrack to the Met. I couldn't wait. Usually I was the "caboose" of the group, but on the way to the Met, I was the leader. This was my Italy, my Sistine Chapel. I wanted to get in and see all that I could take in.

When the four of us entered the building, we knew that our time was limited. There was no way that we were going to be able to see all the art in the building. Even if we could see it all, we wouldn't be able to take it all in. So we decided to divide and conquer, each person going to the section of art that they felt drawn to.

I knew right away where I was headed: European Art. After finding the right elevator and walking through a few of the wrong sections, I ended up at my destination. There were so many paintings, many of them with religious undertones. It was common for the religious leaders to hire painters and sculptors to paint messages from the Bible, so the European Art section was filled with these paintings. I knew that I didn't have a lot of time, so I tried to take as much in as possible.

I wasn't prepared for what I would feel. For instance, I walked up to a painting of Adam and Eve. Between the two people was the beautiful fruit tree with a snake wrapped around the trunk. But as my eyes led upwards on the body of the reptile, I was surprised to find Eve's head at the top of the snake. It startled me. Then it made me a little miffed. *Why was Eve's head on the top of the snake. Oh, I get it, because she ate the apple. What about Adam? He's standing right there. Doesn't he take any responsibility for this?* Then I realized that I was doing it. I was surveying the art, just like I should have been. The art should require me to ask questions, to think about what I'm seeing. The reflection and struggle is what makes art beautiful.

I spent a few minutes with each painting, then moved on to the next. I saw many pictures of women breastfeeding, which I interpreted as giving life. Pictures of people praying, babies with their mothers, and way too many paintings of solemn churches. As I moved on my way, I found myself standing in front of a picture that took my breath away. It was a painting of Jesus being baptized, but it wasn't the usual picture that we see. Growing up, and picture that I had seen of Jesus being baptized included sunny skies, doves, and bright colors. This picture was completely different in its artistic tone. It was painted with dark colors, depicting the baptism at night.

The painting is titled, "The Baptism of Christ" and was painted by Jacopo Bassano. The painting is dark and Christ does not look joyful. It has almost a heavy tone to it. The painting was done in the style of "non finito" which means unfinished. As I read more about the painting, I read that the artist died before the painting was finished, so it truly was "non finito." We will never know what the author wanted to fully do with his piece that he named "The Baptism of Christ." As I looked at the art, I began to become emotional because I knew the rest of the story. Jesus' ministry doesn't end there in what looked like a joyless baptism. There was so much more to his ministry on earth as well as his ultimate act of love and redemption. No, this painting isn't the whole story, it was truly "non finito."

I realized that I was emotional because, I was projecting the painting to my own life. Feeling stuck in a "rut" and not worthy of living out the gifts that God has given to me, I had been discouraged about the things that I wanted to accomplish in life. I looked at the painting and realized that my own story was "non finito." I still had a lot of story left in me. *My* painting was not finished. And a wave of emotion and gratitude washed over me in that building in New York City. God had spoken to my heart through the painting. There is no way that Jacopo Bassano could have known that hundreds of years later, a woman in her mid-thirties would be looking at his painting and contemplating the beauty of life and faith. His painting of Christ's baptism sparked new life within me. I realized in that moment that God has so much more for me and so much more for all of us. We are all "non finito" in some way.

Just like Bassano, Michelangelo could never have guessed what the Sistine Chapel would do for people spiritually. I still have yet to experience it. What I do know, is that God chose ordinary men to live out their gifts and make an incredible impact. If He did it for them, then certainly he wants to do it for us too.

We all have gifts and talents that we have been entrusted with—some artists, musicians, writers, teachers, gardeners, planners, coaches, and so on. Each of us has an area of life that makes us feel alive. That is God's gift to us. What good is a gift if we never use it? If we never share it to others?

Those few hours in New York awakened something inside of me. Something that reminded me that there is more to this story. The best is not behind me—just the opposite, it's before me. Having cancer as a young mother is not the entirety of my story, it's only a small part of my journey.

A couple of years ago, we had a special women's group from Teen Challenge come and perform a concert at our church. There was one woman in the front of the choir who was especially joyful while singing. Her face lit up with every word and you could tell that she was singing from the heart. After the concert was over, I approached the group to thank them for their gift of music. Then I turned to the woman who I had noticed singing with such passion and I said, "You were made to sing." Her eyes welled up with tears and she responded with, "All my life, I've wanted to be a singer. And now I get to sing for God." This woman, who no doubt had experienced tremendous adversity in her life, was now using her gifts to worship God and bless others.

In the words of U2, sometimes we can get "stuck in a moment, and we can't get out of it." When we are stuck in the grit of life, we have a hard time recognizing that there is more life to live and more gifts to share.

We are all unfinished in some way. It's part of life. Don't get "stuck in a moment." Embrace being "non finito" and remember that there is more to each of our stories.

Chapter Seven: I Spy a Veteran

There is a thin line that separates laughter and pain, comedy and tragedy, humor and hurt." Erma Bombeck

I was raised in a very patriotic home. Being in military family is unique. As kids, we got used to our dad disappearing for six months out of the year. We understood that our dad missed our birthdays and Christmas celebrations because he was protecting our country, and we accepted that we could only talk to him on occasion, because that's just part of the gig of being a military kid. It wasn't easy.

I remember when my dad would return from deployment, we would get up early in the morning and head down to the dock to watch for the first sign of his ship. Though the kids were excited to see their dads, the wives were especially excited to have their husbands home. When my dad's ship got close enough, I would squint my eyes to see if I could just catch a glimpse of him on the deck. And then it happened. I would see that face in the crowd that I recognized. My dad. He walked down the ramp with his seabag over his shoulder and we would all run to hug him. Every time he returned from a deployment, I would cry. As a young girl, I couldn't figure out why I would cry on such a happy day. I understand now that my joy was so great, it just spilled out of me. I couldn't contain it. The reunions made my soul burst with joy.

I loved spending time with my dad watching movies. He loved watching John Wayne save the world, so I would sit on the couch and watch John Wayne. My dad was a chief in the Navy. He lived, breathed, and slept the Navy life. Even when we did our chores at home, my dad would refer to the kitchen floor as the "deck." He couldn't help it. It's what he loved.

He was always compassionate towards other people. There were many holidays where my dad would invite sailors without families to our home to enjoy a home-cooked meal. Many of the sailors were far from home and it had been ages since they shared a meal around a table. We were raised to acknowledge that being a service member was a great honor and that our service members were due great respect for their sacrifice. And you know my dad was right. I have carried that in to my home, as well.

I started a small ritual of saying "Thank you" every time I saw a service member. At first it felt a little weird walking up to a stranger and saying thank you, but the more I did it, the better it felt. It was my small gesture to say, I'm grateful. Years and years have gone by and I've kept up with this tradition. My kids are used to me disappearing for a moment to thank a person in the line behind me, or tapping the shoulder of a stranger in the bookstore. You might wonder how I know people are in the service. I know that they are veterans because they wear veterans' hats. Well, 99% of the time they are veterans. One time I thanked a guy and he admitted that he got the hat from Goodwill. Impostor.

I've had all sorts of reactions from service members when I thank them. Most are humbled and grateful, but some get emotional. Some (mostly Vietnam veterans) carry deep wounds of coming back to a nation that didn't thank them. In fact, they were blamed, mistreated, and ignored. I find it especially important to thank those veterans. A couple of years ago, we were at Costco and I saw a sweet older gentleman with his veteran's hat on. I told my husband that I would be right back. I walked up to the gentleman and said, "Sir, I just wanted to say thank you for your service to our country. It really means a lot." He looked at me with kind eyes and said, "I know you're thankful, honey, you told me yesterday at Target." I don't think I have ever been so embarrassed. Seriously..what are the chances that I would thank the same veteran two days in a row? Then I got to thinking about it. If I was going to make a mistake, it's best that I did it trying to be nice about something. You better believe that every time I thank a veteran now, I look really closely at their face to see if I've already thanked them. I've only had one repeat.

I could have chosen to beat myself up over

that, or stop my tradition, but why? Because I made a mistake? I firmly believe that for some reason, we have forgotten the art of laughing at ourselves. Sometimes life is funny, and we make mistakes, but we have to learn accept it and laugh a little.

There's only been one time when my husband told me that he had to draw the line on thanking veterans. We were on a road trip and pulled over in a small town to get some Taco Bell and use the bathroom. Really, I just had to use the bathroom, but I bought a burrito so that I wouldn't feel guilty. I digress.

I hopped out of the car and started my way into Taco Bell when I saw the man in the truck next to me was wearing a veteran's hat. He looked like he could be Willie Nelson's twin. So in a moment of "living the tradition" I knocked on the guy's truck window. He looked over at me with a confused look. I gave him the international signal for roll down your window—I moved my fist in a circular motion imitating the action of manually unrolling a window. He reached over and unrolled his window and I started in thanking him for his service. He heard me out and when I finished, he looked at me, looked at the steering wheel, looked back at me and in a Southern drawl said, "Right on!"

When I got back into the car, my husband said, "That's it. I'm drawing the line. You cannot knock on people's doors or windows to thank them. Even IF you see the hat." I laughed at how ridiculous I must have looked. But that "Right on" has stuck with me for a long time. No, "right on" to you, Willie, and thank you for your service!

———

It didn't take me long to get used to being bald. Truly that look was in when Sinead O'Connor hit the charts with "Nothing Compares 2 U." I guess my cancer was a little behind the times. Every day before I left the house, I would make sure that I either had my wig or my head wrap with me. The head wrap was kind of like a sarong for your skull. I would wrap it around about 5 times and tie it in a knot. It was very bohemian looking.

One great thing about having a wig is that my hair was always done perfectly. Highlights never grew out, curls never fell out, and my hair never frizzed. All day long, my hair looked perfect. The downside of a wig was that in the middle of summer, my head was hot as Hades under that perfectly coiffed hair. It's a weird feeling to know that I was sweating so bad that I worried my wig might shift—or even slip off of my head.

So to combat that I would take my wig off to let my scalp get some air. Not a big deal, right? Well, I guess it was to my husband. He told me that I didn't have any "wig etiquette." I didn't realize that people didn't do well when I would whip my wig off. Honestly, I wasn't thinking of them. I was thinking of my perspiring head. Hot head at the bank? No problem. I'd whip my wig off and fan my head (sometimes with the wig). Sweaty scalp in the grocery store line? Off with the hair. A few minutes of natural air conditioning. Traffic on I-405. Who needs the wig then? I didn't really care where I was, I just wanted relief. Now that I think back about it, people must have been shocked. If I was wearing my wrap at least they would have some warning. If I was in my wig, it might have been a bit startling to see me unexpectedly take my hair off. If I didn't have wig etiquette then, I wonder how bad I'll be with dentures. Oy Vey!

During the chemotherapy treatments, my body started to break down because of all of the poison running through my veins. In addition to losing my hair, my immune system took a nosedive. My white blood cells were not reproducing themselves fast enough for me to continue my treatment. At one point the doctors considered postponing my treatment if my white cells didn't improve before my next chemotherapy appointment. I did not want to add any more "life" time to the cancer, so when my treatments were postponed, I was incredibly discouraged. There was one thing that the doctors could do to ensure that I would be ready for my chemotherapy. They sent me home with Neupogen shots.

Neupogen is a drug that helps the body mass produce white blood cells. The shot itself doesn't hurt, but the process of mass-producing bloods cells can be painful. Waves of pain shot up my back intermittently causing my back to seize. The other thing that I remember about the shots was that my husband had to administer them. The direction from the doctor was for Jeff to find a fatty place on the body, grab the fat, and inject the Neupogen into the body. My husband knew how much I struggled with my postpartum body. I had gained weight and lost hair, not the best combo. At night, before bed, I would go into the kitchen so he could give me the shot. Night after night, Jeff went through this routine of "trying" to find a fatty place on my body. He would carefully survey my stomach—no, not there. Then we would move to my thighs, can't find any fat there. Then to my backside—hmm, not there either. My arms—well, it won't be easy. I knew he was trying to be nice, but honestly, there was tons of fat to choose from and I just wanted to get the shot over with. But I played along; allowing him to, night after night, "search" for a fatty place on my body.

We laugh at those stories now. Laughter truly can be medicine. Sometimes life squeezes us so tightly on both sides that we need relief, and that relief can be found in laughter. Kids offer plenty of opportunities for laughter in our lives.

I'll never forget the time I had a guest in our front room. I had meticulously cleaned the house (we don't really do drop-ins, please give a ten minute warning) for this guest. She was actually coming over to talk about a possible job opportunity. In the middle of our conversation, my daughter came through the front door, walked over to the couch and said, "Mom, you forgot to pick me up at school again." I was mortified. For the record, I didn't forget to pick her up. I'm not saying that I've never forgotten, but that time was legit. She misunderstood the instructions from the morning, which we figured out long after my guest had left, when I couldn't redeem myself.

Kids will say funny things. Unfortunate things will happen. Life is fickle. Sometimes we have to roll with it. But if we take it all so seriously, we will begin to crack. Certainly there are times to be serious and heavy, but one way to combat being overwhelmed is by understanding the gift of laughter. Now go out and thank a veteran.

Chapter Eight: Volleyball, Tattoos, and The Little Engine That Could

"One who gains strength by overcoming obstacles possesses the only strength which can overcome adversity."
Albert Schweitzer

Make a fist. Poke in veins, chemotherapy, scans. The routine was all too familiar. I couldn't wait to be finished. Finally the day had arrived. My last chemotherapy treatment.

I was elated. Done. Finito! The grand finale. Well, that's what I thought. My oncologist wanted to run a few tests to make sure that the cancer was gone. The results were not what I wanted to hear. There was a mass in my chest that they could not identify; it was either scar tissue or more cancer. So, I had another choice to make. We could call it quits on more treatment hoping it was scar tissue and walk out, or I could have the mass radiated for 30 days to shrink it (if it was actually a tumor). Every fiber in my being wanted to be done. The finish line had just been stretched out before me like taffy on a wheel. The end now seemed so far off in the distance.

I had one question for the doctor. "What gives me the most time with my kids?" Without hesitation, he recommended that I continue with the radiation treatment. You might be thinking, its only one more month, but the reality is that I had willed myself to get to the end of the chemo. Another thirty days felt like nothing short of a lifetime.

That night we went home and I went into the bathroom to grieve in private. I was mad at God. I felt that I had done my time. I was angry that I wasn't finished. I started in on the "Why me" in

life. My praying became very real. I was heartbro-
ken. In those moments of sobbing and crying I was
able to let every emotion go out to God: anger, frustration, sadness. Then when I calmed down, I started to feel a peace that I could not quite explain.
Then something was revealed to my soul. I felt like
God was saying to me, Trina, whether you live or
you die, it doesn't change my love for you. I am still
your God.

It was then that I was reminded that I was
not walking this journey alone. Often people ask
me my feelings on why I got cancer. If I'm such a
good person, why didn't God prevent it? I know
this much is true, God didn't give me cancer. Our
bodies get sick, they break down. Some get colds,
some have chronic pain, I had cancer. Though I believe that God didn't give me cancer, I know that
He used that time to teach me a lot about life, faith,
and perseverance. I am a different person because
of the cancer experience.

So another challenge was in front of me. I
had thirty more days to endure treatment. That
night I went to bed emotionally and physically exhausted. But you know what they say, joy comes in
the morning. Every day brings a new perspective …

and the next day things seemed a little brighter.

Radiation was not as difficult as the chemotherapy in some ways. It didn't take the physical
toll on my body and it didn't take that long to have
the actual treatment. The only drawback was that I
had to go every day, with breaks on the weekend.

I was nervous on the first day of my radiation treatment. The treatment required me to re-
move my shirt and my bra and lay on a table so
doctors could measure and mark the exact lines for
the radiation on my chest. Let's just stop and take in
the moment. Lying down without a shirt and bra is
the most humiliating position. Gravity only goes
one way, and my body wasn't too many months
post-partum. To top it off, I had a doctor measuring
and marking my skin like he was getting ready to
build the Empire State Building on my chest. His
plans were impeccable.

The next day I returned for my first actual
radiation treatment. Before they took me into the
room, I had to get my radiation tattoos. Say that
again? Yes, my radiation tattoos. That was news to
me. In order for the doctors to identify the point of
radiation, they needed to put two tattoos on my

chest. The tattoos were just little dots, but they were forever dots. I would have rather had a flower than two obscure ink dots. They are still there and one is visible when I wear v-neck shirts.

Years later, my husband and I were attending a gala and a woman came up to me and started chatting. She had had a few too many glasses of wine when she said, "Oh my goodness, you have marked yourself with a pen." She licked her thumb (like my grandma used to do when I was a kid) and rubbed it against my skin, trying to rub off the pen/tattoo. I had to laugh at the situation because I knew that if I told her what it was, I would have to go into the whole cancer story. So I just chalked it up to silly me, I inked myself on my chest again.

The whole procedure for the radiation took less than ten minutes. I had to go in the dressing room, take off my shirt and my bra, climb on the silver table, and watch as a huge robotic machine hovered over me, then everyone would scatter from the room so they could radiate me. I always thought that was weird, people would run for cover, but assured me that I would be fine. The biggest obstacle I had on the first day was walking into the radiation room and exposing my chest. Remember friends, I had just had a baby months before. My body was in reshaping mode. On day one, I had to be coaxed out of the dressing room—embarrassed that everyone was going to see me topless again. Day after day, it was the same routine. Each day, I got less and less embarrassed. In fact, when I got closer to day thirty, I felt like I was taking my shirt off in the parking lot, somersaulting over the waiting room chairs, kicking in the radiation door, flipping up onto to the radiation table and pushing the button myself. Parkour cancer-mom. Not really, but I did get over being naked and radiated day after day.

Every appointment was a step closer to the finish line. Something to hope for. Something to cling to. Forever was within my reach.

———

This past year, my daughter signed up to play volleyball. Now, bless her heart, she is slightly more athletic than her mama. I lettered in high school for keeping score for the volleyball team. True story. My dad was so proud that he bought me a letterman's jacket. So I have a big blue jacket with a single white volleyball for keeping score. Athletic,

I was not.

But my daughter just might have gotten her dad's athletic abilities (he did play semi-pro hockey). She signed up and we got her all the gear she needed; the uniform, socks, and the kneepads. Kate worked really hard to perfect her game. She always cheered her teammates on and played with enthusiasm. The one thing that she could not master was her serve technique. Time after time, she would serve with enthusiasm, but the ball would smack into the net. I watched from the stands, as she would see the ball fall to the ground. As her mom, I knew her disappointment ran deep, but she kept a smile on her face. Game after game, the same scenario repeated itself. She'd serve, the ball would hit the net and fall to the ground. Whenever Kate got up to serve, everyone would cheer her on—her teammates, the parents, heck—even the other teams were pulling for her. Then it happened. One of her games she walked up to the line, bounced the ball, a few times, lifted her arm and smacked that ball. In slow motion, I watched the ball fly up. Secretly I was calculating the velocity, speed, and depth—or whatever. I just wanted to make sure that it cleared the net. And that it did. The ball sailed over the net and landed between two players on the other team. My daughter had just scored her first point.

I had a huge celebration on the sideline. I jumped up and shouted, "That's my girl." I was so happy for her because I knew she was happy.

I believe that's how God interacts with us. When we are sad, it breaks his heart. When we are joyful, he too is celebrating. The truth is, that even if Kate didn't make the serve, it would never change how I feel about her. She is the light in a dark room, she's the kid who has empathy for every lost kitten, and she is a natural writer with a witty sense of humor. She's my girl. Serve or no serve, I love her exactly as she is.

Sometimes when life gets tough, it's hard to believe that God sees what we're going through. A couple of months ago, I was struggling through a very difficult season of life. I felt disconnected from God- overwhelmed and discouraged. I decided to get up early one morning and just spend some quiet time alone with God. I opened my Bible and read through a few chapters. I read Psalm 27:13, "I remain confident of this: I will see the goodness of the Lord in the land of the living."

Something about that verse jumped out at me. It was strange. I just kept reading it to myself, over and over. I was reminded that God's goodness would be evident in my life even through this difficult situation. After I spent a few minutes in prayer, I decided to put my Bible down and pick up my computer to check my email. I was thrilled to see an email from a dear friend in Tennessee. Nothing could have prepared me for what I read next. She sent an email sending her best to me through this season of struggle. She said that she felt that she should share Psalm 27:13 with me. *"I remain confident of this: I will see the goodness of the Lord in the land of the living."*

I was shocked. How in the world could she have known that I was just reading that very same verse? She didn't, but God did. I truly believe that God gives us signs that he sees what we are dealing with. This was His way of showing me that He was present in those moments.

Sometimes we just need that reminder that in the adversity of life, God is there and we can continue to press on. It isn't easy, but a moment isn't forever.

Like Kate persevered to get that ball over the net, I had to persevere day after day to finish my treatments. There were so many times when I wanted to throw in the towel, sit in the corner, and cry. But it was important for me to finish, to give the treatment my best shot. On that last day of treatment, I buttoned my shirt, picked up my purse, and walked out of the treatment center, not wanting to look back. Finishing that final treatment was my volleyball serve over the net, my moment to shine, my invitation to exhale.

Chapter Nine: 1865

"Give me your eyes for just one second,
Give me your eyes so I can see
Everything that I've been missing
Give me Your love for humanity." Brandon Heath-
Give Me Your Eyes

Many people know The Salvation Army as a chain of thrift stores where you can score a deal on a brand name pair of jeans or pick up a board game for a quarter. Some know The Salvation Army as a group of people playing brass instruments or ringing the bell at the kettle during Christmas time, extending a hand to the poor. Most do not realize that The Salvation Army is also a church. I always thought that was strange that more people didn't know this considering the name includes the word "Salvation." I grew up attending a Salvation Army church, learning about Jesus, learning to play the cornet, and ringing the bell during Christmas. I rarely told people where I went to church because some would tease me about attending church in a thrift store. Of course we didn't meet in the thrift store, but I didn't have the tools to stick up for myself. It wasn't until much later in life that I realized that being raised in The Salvation Army church played a huge part in my spiritual formation and my passion for social justice.

William and Catherine Booth started The Salvation Army to meet the needs of people, spiritually and physically. They knew that God's love was a gift for all people, but it seemed that the poor and marginalized were not being welcomed in the churches with the rest of society. This stood out as an injustice to William and Catherine. They knew that their calling was to minister to the poor and to show love to a hurting world. That meant everyone—especially those that were looked down on by the church—prostitutes, alcoholics, homeless, and children starving on the streets. The Booths shared God's love by meeting people right where they were, even in the gutters. You can imagine how scandalous this must have been in London in 1865. The Booths were pulling people out of the grit of life and bringing them into physical and spiritual health—preaching that God's grace was for everyone.

The Salvation Army was also cutting edge in getting children out of matchmaking factories, feeding the homeless, and standing against every social injustice. The word spread, The Army grew, and people became empowered to share Jesus' love with others.

You still see it today. When a disaster strikes, you see the big Red Shield and a Salvation Army Officer close by handing out cups of hot coffee. *A Heart to God, and a Hand to Man.*

I didn't realize the rich spiritual heritage that I was a part of, but God knew. The more I learned about the founders of The Salvation Army, the more I realized that the most courageous (and out of the box) people in the world are the ones who see a need and do what it takes to stand up and make a difference. They choose to make a difference even when it isn't popular or comfortable and sometimes when it isn't safe. You have those same kind of people in your own communities, it's the PTA mom who brings a group of students together to collect food for the homeless, it's the group of high school students who form groups to stand against bullying, it's the local church that raises awareness and funds to fight human trafficking.

The truth is that we all have the ability to make a difference, whether we want to admit it or not. We see things in this world that drive us crazy, challenge us, break our hearts, inspire us, and put fire in our bones. We want to do something. We want to respond. We want to fight back, but sometimes we don't. We talk ourselves out of the extraordinary because we feel like we are too ordinary. If I were to ask any one of these heroes of the faith, if they were setting out to build a movement, or become something great, I'm sure their answer would be no. They were just humbly meeting a need.

Helen Keller said it best. *"I am only one, but*

still I am one. I cannot do everything, but still I can do something; and because I cannot do everything, I will not refuse to do something that I can do."

I have been on the receiving end of this kind of kindness and response.

Going through the cancer was difficult in a number of ways. Aside from the being sick and bald, we also had to deal with the financial repercussions of cancer. It was so expensive to be sick ... and insurance only covered so much. The reality was that we were a young family trying to "make it," with the added pressure of oncology bills. We were at the point of breaking and we didn't have enough money to make our monthly bill for my health insurance.

Throughout scripture, I would read how God as the great provider. *"That is why I tell you not to worry about everyday life—whether you have enough food and drink, or enough clothes to wear. Isn't life more than food, and your body more than clothing? Look at the birds. They don't plant or harvest or store food in barns, for your heavenly Father feeds them. And aren't you far more valuable to him than they are? Can all your worries add a single moment to your life?"* Matthew

That verse was easy to read and accept when life was going well. Of course, I need not worry about my life; God was in every step, right? It's when the grit of life poured in that I start looking at scripture differently. I searched the scripture for hope and meaning. I read verses about provision— and cried out to God. *Do you see me? Do you know that I can't pay my health insurance premium, let alone my medical bills? I need this treatment to survive!*

My prayers were raw and heartfelt, but in all honesty, my trust that God *would* provide was half-hearted. I just didn't see a way out of our financial hole.

Living in Southern California promised blue skies and hot summers. We lived in a small apartment in San Diego. Because of cost, we rarely ran our air conditioning unit. Sitting in the apartment on a hot day with two children was a struggle. On especially hot days, my husband and I would take the kids to the local mall and enjoy their free air conditioning. We didn't have money to spend, but with the kids in the double stroller, it gave us a few hours to just walk and talk. One Saturday, Jeff and I were walking around the mall talking about life, treatments, and bills. We decided to stop by Hot Dog on a Stick and get a corn dog for Caleb. During those hot summer months, I usually wore a wrap on my head—it was much cooler than a wig. There I stood with my wrap on my head, my two kids in the stroller, waiting for a corn dog. Sometimes I would catch people staring at me. There was always an awkward moment when our eyes would meet and instantly they would redirect their eyes away, feeling caught. I could tell that they wondered about my illness, and why I had a wrap on my head. Unless they asked me directly, I pretended that everything was normal.

Jeff scouted a table for us and saved our spot. I ordered lunch and made my way back to the table. I didn't even sit down before Jeff told me that a lady approached him asking if I was his wife. Jeff (who was protective of me and my feelings) said that I was. The lady asked Jeff to give me her card. While Jeff was telling me this, I asked him to point the lady out to me.

I navigated my way through the busy food court and walked to the stranger's table to introduce myself. "My husband said that you stopped by our table and asked about me. How can I help you?" Sheepishly the woman replied, "I saw you over there with your two children, and I noticed the wrap on your head. Years ago, I had cancer when my two children were small. When I saw you, my heart just went out to you. After I went into remission, I decided to start a skin care business for people going through chemotherapy." Instantly I thought she was trying to sell me something. We talked a little more and she asked how I was doing. Jeff joined in on the conversation. It was nice to talk to someone who had experienced what I was experiencing. At the end of our conversation, she asked me if she could send a few skin cares samples to my home. I don't usually give out my home address to strangers, but for some reason, I felt a connection with her, almost like a cancer survivor mentorship.

She wished me the best of luck and we went on our way. I was actually encouraged by the conversation. It reminded me that everyone has a story. You never really know what people have been through until they share it.

A few days later, a box was delivered to our door. At first, I didn't recognize the address, then it hit me. This was from my new friend from the mall.

I opened it expecting to find some sample skin care packets. Instead, I found 8 new bottles of skin care products; cleansers, moisturizers, and toners. Full bottles! There had to have been over a hundred dollars worth of products. At the bottom of the box was an envelope. Inside the envelope was a check for $500.

As if that wasn't enough to shock me, wrapped around the check was a letter stating; "... from my skincare business, I started a foundation. My foundation would like to pay your health insurance premiums for the next six months." I reread the sentence a few times to make sure that I comprehended it correctly. I couldn't imagine why a complete stranger would be so giving. Her radical generosity changed my reality. I sat down, stunned, and broke into tears.

God did see me. He knew what I needed and He provided in His time and in His way. I didn't know how we were going to pay for our insurance, but I'll tell you this much, I never thought that God would answer my prayers, by meeting a stranger, on a hot day, in the food court.

That woman was incredibly influential in my

life. Her generosity changed my reality.

You too are influential. You might not think so, but you are. You might be reading this in your nightgown after a long day of chasing kids. You are influential. Perhaps you've been in board meetings all day working on policies with your Board of Directors. You are influential. Maybe you're reading this book on your lunch break during the graveyard shift. You are influential.

Influencers are people who realize that they are only one, but that they are still one. They can't do everything, but they can do something. That is you. Right now. Right where you are.

My friend Stacy is an incredible person. She is the person responsible for giving me great haircuts and colors. Sitting in Stacy's chair is a little bit like a vacation from life. We shoot the breeze, talk about our kids, and look through the latest *People* magazine together. I comment on the magazine articles while she paints my hair with color. Stacy is an amazing hairdresser.

But there is more to Stacy's story. She is not just a hairdresser with two kids, a husband, and a family dog. She is an activist and a world changer in our community. Six years ago, Stacy's youngest son had a sore on his cheek that wouldn't go away. After a few weeks, Stacy took Ethan to the doctors to have it checked out. That led to a string of appointments, tests, and ultimately specialists. The string of appointments led to the words every mom is terrified of hearing, "We're sorry, but it's cancer." In an instant, her son transitioned from carefree little boy to cancer patient. Her world was turned upside-down. Our community watched as Shawn and Stacy traveled to get their son the treatment that he needed. Stacy balanced his care, her job, and her family. Ethan endured his treatment and went into remission. After six months, the cancer returned, and Ethan courageously fought it for a second time.

Ethan is in remission and returning to a life of "normalcy," going to school, playing with friends, and mastering levels of his video games. But the experience has forever changed their family. The whole experience put "fire in her bones." Stacy became an activist to raise awareness for childhood cancer. She has educated thousands in our community. The once-shy hairdresser now finds herself giving speeches in front of hundreds, hosting fundraisers for Cookies for Kids' Cancer, and she participates in radio-thons for St. Jude's Hospital. She is determined to do her part to fight cancer for kids.

Stacy is an influencer. She didn't start out that way and she never would have wished to go through the experience, but just like Helen Keller, Stacy "will not refuse to do something that she can do." I have a feeling that Stacy and Helen would have been good friends.

We are the most influential when we are not focused on ourselves. It's true. Look at the people who have made the greatest difference in this world, it's usually because they are focusing on something much bigger than themselves.

We are influential in our own ways, within our own circles, and at just the right time. Sometimes it's as big a starting a movement, but often it's in the small moments of life. The poignant moments when we can encourage with a word of kindness, a moment of silence, or an act of love.

When our kids were small, my husband and I spent a summer living in Juneau, Alaska. Southeast Alaska is a beautiful place. The lush green trees grow right alongside clear blue glaciers that shoot into the open. You can't help but feel small in Alaska, knowing that what you're seeing is undoubtedly the work of a majestic creator.

During our time in Juneau, we decide to take a trip to Anchorage. Trip is an understatement; it was more of a journey. The trip meant 6 hours on a crowded ferry ride followed by a two-day trip up through the Yukon. Throw in two small kids, an over-packed car, and a husband who loves to sightsee … it wasn't an ideal trip. But of course, we tried to make the best of it. And the best of it started at 5 a.m. in the morning as we packed the car for the trip. The car was supposed to be packed the night before, but being in bear country, my husband did not want to pack the car in the dark, so we packed it in the morning.

As we made our way to the minivan, we were greeted with a trail of what looked like clumps of snow. Snow in the summer in Juneau? My eyes were playing tricks on me…or not. The "snow" was actually clumps of chewed up dirty diapers from our large trash bin. In the middle of the night, a very smart bear figured out how to unlock the bear-proof trash locker by our house. It was in that locker that we had four bags of trash waiting to be picked up. At the time we had two kids in diapers. It was a week's worth of trash; I'll let you do the math. That makes for a lot of "snow." You can imagine how irritated I was to get up early in the morning, make my way to the car with all of the luggage and car seats in tow to be greeted with a trail of smelly trash. Not the best way to start a trip.

Within an hour the car was packed and we were ready to embark on our Alaskan Canadian adventure. First stop, the ferry. The kids were really too young to understand how cool it was to be boarding the ferry with our car. With the guidance of the ferry worker, we pulled the van in close to the car in front of us, put the car in park and gathered our items to enjoy the six-hour ferry ride. Once we climbed the stairs to the main deck, we realized that this was no cruise line. The ferry reminded me of the "Greyhound" of the seas. Our particular ferry was packed to the brim with people sitting on the floor, some sleeping and some playing cards to pass time. Jeff and I knew that in order to find a seat, we would have to separate. He took one child and I took the other. Kate, who was three at the time, and

I headed over to the only two seats that I saw were available. Unfortunately, they were right next to a man who looked like he had been on the ferry and without a shower for some time. His beard was greasy, his hair unkempt, and the smell of stale odor emanated from his body. I was not too thrilled about sitting next to him.

I asked the gentleman if the seats next to him were reserved. He glanced over at me and in a quiet voice told me that we were welcome to sit there. I thanked him and sat down in the seat closest to him. I put Kate on the other side of me and dug through the diaper bag to find some crackers and coloring crayons to keep her busy.

Kate had no interest in the treasures I was pulling out from the diaper bag. She couldn't keep her eyes off of the stranger sitting on the other side of me. The more I tried to distract her, the more she kept glancing over to the gentleman next to me.

Every mom knows that there is a "go to" stash of goodies for kids; cheerios, fish crackers, graham cracker—and for the most desperate moments, M&M's. I tried to distract Kate with coloring crayons and food, but she was more interested in staring at the stranger next to me. I started to get nervous worrying about the words that might come out of her mouth, such as a statement about his personal hygiene. "He smells mommy? He needs a bath." But I couldn't be more wrong. My little girl, with her big brown eyes, looked that man straight in the face and said, "Hi Jesus!" The man looked back at Kate, then at me. He put his head down and said, "That is the nicest thing anyone has ever said to me."

My little girl didn't see the greasy beard, or the worn out clothes. She saw Jesus. In that moment, she taught me a huge lesson about how I see people—the snap judgments, misconceptions, and stereotypes. I was guilty of answering a thousand questions in my head, before I even began a conversation.

Kate reminded me that a true conversation can only begin when we see Jesus in others. Kate was influential in helping me gain a different perspective in how I see people. Oh, I knew that she probably thought he looked like Jesus because his long hair resembled some pictures in church, but I didn't want to miss the deeper meaning by explaining away her greeting.

Think about your sphere of influence. Truly it's much bigger than you realize—your family, your neighbors, your friends at work? It's all the people that you are in relationship with. The things that you say and the things that you do influence this group of people. This naturally leads me to the next question. What are the issues in this world that put "fire in your bones"? For my daughter, it would be anything that has to do with animals. For me it's anything to do with oppression of women and human trafficking. When I hear of those issues, something deep inside my soul stirs. There's an ache of injustice that breaks my heart, and I am instantly compelled to see how I can do something to make a difference.

Once you realize that you are influential and that you recognize what you are passionate about, it's time to take action.

"Fire in our bones" does nothing unless we put action to our feet. This is the point where people become overwhelmed. Sometimes it seems like the problems of this world are so deep and great that there's no way that we will be able to do anything of significance to help. Don't allow yourself to get stuck there.

For almost every cause, there is an organization designed to give you tools and opportunities to serve. You don't have to build the whole system, you just have to find likeminded people and organizations—then start small.

As I mentioned, I have a heart to see the end of human trafficking, so I researched some organizations to see how I could become a little more involved. I quickly realized that education and awareness was needed in our area. There were many people in my community who didn't even know about human trafficking, or they assumed it was a problem in another country.

I realized that the first step of action was to gather a group of women and talk about human trafficking locally, domestically, and globally. I put the word out on Facebook. Nine women showed up that night. I showed a short video about human trafficking. We talked about issues in our own area. The discussion prompted many ideas on how we could be more proactive in our own community as well as raise awareness on a greater level. We discussed the ways that we could get involved and make a difference.

We can all take small steps to get involved and make a positive change in this world; and in the process of making a difference you will be influencing your family, friends, and coworkers to see a greater picture of what they can do to make a difference.

In the grit of life, your voice is needed. Just like the young couple in London, England who had a heart for the poor, the Parent Teacher Association collecting food for the homeless, the local mom fighting to find a cure for cancer, or the little girl on the ferry sharing words of encouragement—remember that you can make a difference. Miracles can happen anywhere—even in the mall at Hot Dog on a Stick.

Chapter Ten: Stops Along the Way

"We come with beautiful secrets, We come with purposes written on our hearts, written on our souls. We come to every new morning, with possibilities only we can hold." Sara Groves- *Add to the Beauty*

We are a traveling family. I am so thankful that my kids are very good travelers in the car. I've heard stories from other parents who are forced to stop every 30 minutes due to carsickness. Fortunately our kids seem to hold their own in the car. Every year we embark on a 14-hour trip from Northern California to Southern California. It's amazing to think that you can travel for that long and still be in the same state—and that's not even border-to-border.

Of course we don't do the whole trip in one day, we break it up with a stop in between. Everything is defined by that stop. How far to Sacramento? When will we get to Sacramento?

Life is divided by similar stops. On the roadmap of life, we have stops that define our journey—graduation, career, marriage, birth of children, and so on. It's not that we have the same stops in life, it's that we think that we are able to anticipate some of our stops. We try our best to predict our roadmap, but the reality is, there are some stops that we will not anticipate; the death of a loved one, bankruptcy, sickness, depression, and divorce. The unexpected stops on our journey.

Those stops will be there whether we like them or not. I know the exact date that I was diagnosed with cancer. I remember where I was when I was told. I remember how I felt. I remember it all. It's a stop I didn't anticipate, and yet I intimately know every detail of the experience.

Just as the diagnosis was a stop I wasn't prepared for, so was the day that I was told I was in remission. It couldn't anticipate how it would feel to hear the "second chance" news. The cancer was no longer in my system. I had been given a new start—every dream in life was now possible. It was surreal to think that in less than a year, my life went from walking through hell to pure joy! The interesting thing is that I had perfect health before the cancer, but I didn't recognize or even acknowledge it. I took it for granted. It was the hell of cancer that made me truly understand the beauty of life. Adversity has a way of helping us understand the difference between the important and the petty.

The cancer taught me that life can (and will) be filled with brokenness. That we will journey through experiences bigger than ourselves. We will have to lean on friends and admit that we need help. We will have honest and raw conversations with God. That date of diagnosis will be a permanent road stop in my life map, but I also have a remission date. That date represents the hope for something better, the process of healing, and the celebration of life. I could have never anticipated that defining moment. I often wonder, if I hadn't experienced the cancer, would I ever have really appreciated life?

My cancer had officially ended, but that didn't mean that the journey was over. I still had to deal with the fallout that cancer brought into my world. On a physical level, my body had to learn how to heal and rebuild. Slowly my hair started to return. My family had to learn a new normal, one that we welcomed. We got used to feeling healthier and enjoying life with our two sweet kids.

My emotional journey took a little longer. I dealt with a lot of guilt over taking the chemotherapy with Kate. Logically, I knew that it was the best shot that I could give for Kate and I to live, but emotionally, I still couldn't reconcile that I intentionally hurt my daughter. I carried that guilt around for a long time and I allowed it to take root in my heart. The problem is when we carry anything around in secret, we give it the opportunity to fester and metastasize inside. What was happening in my experience was that every time I saw or read anything in the news about moms who hurt their children, I would think to myself, *You're no different ... you took chemotherapy with Kate.*

I was so ashamed of the way I felt. I didn't want anyone to know that I was struggling with those feelings.

One night, I was watching the news and a story came on about a mother who abused her kids. I instantly started crying and I said to Jeff, "I'm so sorry for what I did. I would never intentionally hurt our kids." Jeff had no idea where all of those emotions were coming from. He held me in his arms as I explained my hidden shame. We both knew that my decision was made with good intentions, but it was clear that I needed to see someone professionally to work out the emotions attached.

I journeyed into a counselor's office so that I could work through some of the fallout of being sick and taking chemotherapy while I was pregnant. The therapist was gentle in allowing me to cry my way through my emotions. And then she responded with something that changed my perspective forever. She said, "Trina, if you went to the dentist and he drilled on a healthy tooth for no reason, that would be a bad hurt. But if you went to the dentist with a cavity and he drills on the right tooth, so that he can fill it to make it stronger, that's a good hurt. When you took chemotherapy during your pregnancy ... that was a good hurt." I know it probably makes sense to the rest of you, but for me I needed to hear those words. I needed to know that I wasn't a terrible mom. I needed to know that I made a good decision in the impossible predicament of being pregnant with cancer.

When I share my story at women's retreats and conferences, I often talk about my time in counseling. For some reason there is a lot of shame around mental health, counseling, and medication. We need to change the stigma around mental health issues. People need to understand that life is tough and everyone needs a "safe space" to work through their issues. I'm an advocate for counseling. I think it's important. Through counseling, I was able to find incredible wisdom and personal freedom. Who wouldn't want that?

Even with counseling, life didn't return to perfect, but it did return to real. We had a new perspective on marriage, parenting, friendships and life in general.

For the first six months after remission, I made Jeff feel every "new" lump on my body. I was convinced that the cancer was waiting for the perfect time to return. My anxiety was over the top. I had regular scans to make sure that I was healthy. Each healthy scan helped my anxiety wane. When I made it to the one year mark of being cancer free, I felt like I had won the lottery. Then I made it to two years, then five, when I could officially announce that I was cured from Hodgkin's Lymphoma. Cured, but forever changed. We settled back into life and my season of cancer was put on a shelf in my mind, like the almost forgotten can of baked beans in the pantry. It's always there, but I don't always think about it.

Five years after the cancer, we completed our family with our youngest son, Noah. We were officially a family of five. Life was again feeling optimistic.

Life and health have not been perfect since my remission. I've had some health issues that are related to my cancer and treatment. Some days I find myself discouraged as I wonder about the uncertainty of my health in the future. I can't stay in that space too long otherwise I begin to deal with mild depression. I have to remember that the gift I have is the gift of today. When I start to feel over-whelmed about the future, I seek perspective from the past.

A few weeks ago, I was going through our picture box and I found a picture of me in a head wrap, standing next to Jeff. In his arms, he held Kate—our precious little girl. I stared at the picture for a few minutes taking it all in. Thinking about everything that has happened in the past 13 years. I remember being so discouraged during that time thinking that I would never get through the treat-ments, but I did. I ran my fingers over the picture caressing the top of my head wrap and then touch-ing the image of our baby. My Kate. My fighter. The picture is just a snapshot. It doesn't tell the whole story. It's "non finito." There is so much more in our lives- more joy, brokenness, faith, laughter, celebra-tion, health issues, healing, just more … life!

All of us have those unexpected moments that have peppered our journeys. Those situations that made us feel like we were hanging on by a thread, and even taking the next breath seems like a chore. But then we have the moments that make us feel lighter than air—that all is right with the world.

And we realize that we are more resilient than we ever thought possible.

Not too far from my house is a 28 mile stretch of road called The Avenue of the Giants. This road weaves in and out of groves of redwood trees. Redwood trees have certain grandeur about them. They don't have to work at being beautiful or majestic—they just are. When I get out of the car and walk among them, I start to realize how small I am. These trees have lived through years of history. They seem greater than life. I look up and keep looking. From the ground, I might never see the top. Every now and then, I have walked past a redwood tree that has been cut at the stump. The circular lines that mark the age of the tree feel like a peek into nature's diary. The lines represent a long life lived, perseverance through floods, fires, and wind. There is strength in the story of a redwood tree. But the greatest part about the redwood stump is the story isn't over. Redwoods trees, when cut down to the stump, will sprout new life.

Life is like that tree. We get cut down—sometime to the stump and we are totally exposed to the elements, but we have resilience—a strength that sprouts new life.

And that new life changes us forever. We will never be the same as before, but we come back with a different perspective. And we realize that we are more tender, more driven, and keenly aware of pain and joy.

What we do with that knowledge and that experience is up to us.

Before the cancer, I always wanted my story to have the shape of perfection. I wanted to have the "American Dream" of having a perfect family, a beautiful home with a white picket fence. Somewhere in the journey of life, I had lost my sense of what was really important. I had lost touch with the tenacious child inside of me who believed that I could do anything, even survive scary bike jumps, and that my dreams were possible. My dreams morphed into what society told me that I should dream.

Let's not be "should-dreamers." There are enough of those in this world. We can break out of the norm and live life to the fullest—in every area of our lives, and in every season.

My battle with cancer taught me that the

most beautiful moments of life can be found everywhere. The moments include friends sharing stories and laughter around the dinner table, watching my kids try something new, taking weekends away to work on my writing, enjoying a lazy Saturday morning with my husband, traveling to new places, chasing life-long dreams, and living with gratitude along the way.

What is something that you have always wanted to do? Run a marathon? Write a book? Organize a food drive? Learn how to play an instrument? Run for local office?

Do it. It's as simple as that. Take a step and do it. Don't wait for something tragic in life to give you the perspective that life is now. Each of us have been given gifts and talents in life—dreams of something more. But sometimes our dreams get pushed aside, put on a shelf, and ignored. No longer! Make a promise to yourself that you will take a step today in moving forward in your dream. Your story is "non finito." You can go anywhere from here. Get on your bike, peddle as fast as you can, and take the jump. The world is waiting for you.

Notes

Chapter One: Taking the Jump!
Information about Harriet Tubman can be found at
www.harriettubman.com
If you are a mother of preschoolers,
check out www.MOPS.org

Chapter Two: The Most Beautiful Stranger
Jeremiah 29:11 The Bible, New International Version

Chapter Three: Hamburger Helper and Half
Marathons
Information about the redwood trees can be found
at www.savetrees.org
Ecclesiastes 4:9-10 The Bible, New International
Version

Chapter Five: Welcome to Life
You can read more about the Chilean Mining incident at: http://topics.nytimes.com/top/reference/
timestopics/subjects/c/chile_mining_acciden-
t_2010/index.html?inline=nyt-classifie

Chapter Six: Jesus in New York

To see the painting The Baptism of Christ painted by Jacopo Bassano, visit this website: http://www.metmuseum.org/collection/the-collection-online/search/440393

Chapter Eight: Volleyball, Tattoos, and The Little Engine That Could

Psalm 27:13 The Bible, New International Version

Chapter Nine: 1865

To learn more about the work and ministry of The Salvation Army, visit this website www.salvation-army.org

To read more about Helen Keller, visit www.hki.org

Matthew 6:25-27 The Bible, New Living Translation

Acknowledgments

I'm so grateful for the people who helped shape this book. This list includes many friends, family, and colleagues who have encouraged me along the way. A special note of thanks to my editor, Carla Foote. I appreciate all of your hard work on this project. This book would not have happened without you. Thank you to all of my readers including Becky, Sharon, Corinne, Mark, Jana, Jennifer, Tracey, Clara, and Heather.

To the organizations mentioned in the book; Mothers of Preschoolers (MOPS), The Salvation Army, Cookies for Kids' Cancer, and all of the other great organizations, thank you for all of the work that you do to make a difference in this world. To the powerful writers, bloggers, and speakers of The Redbud Writers Guild, thank you for your support and encouragement.

I was given permission to use a very special poem titled "I Am" by Michaela Zickuhr. Michaela left this earth at a young age and she is now in the arms of Jesus. Her legacy lives on through the words that she wrote in her poem. Thank you so much, Veronica, for allowing me to reprint her poem in this book. I hope others find encouragement through her words.

Thank you to all the veterans who have served our country. A special note of thanks to my younger brothers, Matt and Dan, for your military service. I appreciate your sacrifice.

A huge amount of gratitude to my parents, Joe and Cathy. Thank you for you giving me a foundation of faith. You were the first to tell me about Jesus. I'm so grateful for your example in my life.

To Jeff, Caleb, Kate, and Noah, thank you for sharing your lives with me.

And finally to all of the people who will read this book, this quote is for you,

Here is the world. Beautiful and terrible things will happen. Don't be afraid.
-Frederick Buechner

About the Author

Trina Pockett is an inspirational writer, speaker, and leader with over fifteen years of experience serving in ministry. She has served in leadership roles within The Salvation Army, MOPS, Stonecroft Ministries, and is currently on staff with Compassion International.

Trina's own story about her battle with cancer reminds her that life is a gift from God. Through storytelling, humor, and encouragement, Trina shares about the incredible adventure of living a life of faith.

She is a member of the Redbud Writer's Guild and her work has been featured in numerous magazines including *Fullfill* Magazine, *Intersections*, and the MOPS International website.

Trina and her family currently reside in beautiful Northern California.

To learn more visit *www.trinapockett.com* or connect with @trinapockett on Twitter.

Made in the USA
Charleston, SC
28 December 2015